OUT OF SUFFERING
INTO GLORY

Susan & Jeremy,
May the Lord bless
your lives and shine
through you to touch
our world.
Love,
Sally Keinan
Psalm 34

OUT OF SUFFERING INTO GLORY

God's Redemptive Purposes for Suffering

Sally Keiran

Out Of Suffering Into Glory

God's Redemptive Purposes For Suffering

Published by Master Press

© 2012 by Sally Keiran
All rights reserved
Cover design by Kim Taylor (kimiweb.com)

Out Of Suffering Into Glory

God's Redemptive Purposes For Suffering
ISBN 978-09885057-1-1

For information:

MASTER PRESS
3405 ISLAND BAY WAY, KNOXVILLE, TN 37931

Mail to: publishing@ masterpressbooks.com

This book is dedicated to the glory of God.
His loving-kindness delivers the humble
out of the kingdom of darkness and brings them
into His glorious Kingdom of light and truth.
Nothing on earth compares to knowing Jesus Christ
and being His beloved son and daughter.

ಐ

Whom have I in heaven but you?
And earth has nothing I desire besides you.
My flesh and my heart may fail,
but God is the strength of my heart
and my portion forever.
Psalm 73:25-26

Acknowledgements

With all my heart I thank my loving husband, Alan, whose encouragement throughout the process of writing this book sustained me and kept me fixed on the goal of getting this message which the Lord gave me into print for those who suffer. I also thank my precious children: my daughter Jennifer with her husband Jason, and my son John, who walked with me through some of the trials I write about in this book. Their love, affirmation and prayers have blessed my life in ways they may never understand. Also my love to our granddaughter Lily whose smiles and hugs gave me joyful reprieve in the midst of the arduous process of writing.

The Lord blessed me with a dear friend and writing coach, Abigail Knutson, who worked with me with great enthusiasm and skill and who affirmed me chapter by chapter with the value of what God had directed me to write. Thank you Abigail. Also thanks to my husband Alan and friend Polly Barlow for reading and critiquing my first draft. I thank God for my friend Joleen Miller, my daughter Jennifer, my sister Irene, my spiritual daughter Johanna, and my Monday prayer group ladies whose prayers sustained me through the many months of this project.

Also thanks to the many friends and family members who are a part of our Dunamis International Ministries prayer team. Your prayers were invaluable in carrying me through the months of writing. I felt your prayers. Thank you.

I also want to acknowledge our dear friends in southeast India who bear testimony to God's redemptive purposes in suffering. The orphans and staff of the Light Home, the widows, lepers and rural pastors are often on my heart. I thank them for what they have taught me of suffering, and the glory of God. May the love of Jesus Christ continue to sustain them and give purpose to their suffering as they live for the glory of God.

Endorsements

"This topic is SO NEEDED in these days, when so many are suffering now in so many ways, and are asking, "Why, God?" Our LORD has graciously allowed Sally and her husband, Alan, to minister into the lives of some of "the least of these" - the outcasts of Indian society who are afflicted with leprosy. In ministering to this community of lepers, Sally has found a pearl of great price: the redemptive plan that Father will bring forth within each of us when He leads us into, and through, a season of suffering. I believe this precious book holds the keys that will help all of us to grow and mature in the things of God during times of suffering and affliction."

Sara Ballenger,
Founder, Capitol Hill Prayer Partners

"Sally Keiran's book, *Out of Suffering into Glory*, examines the question that confronts everyone at some point in their life: why am I (or my spouse, friend, child) suffering? Or perhaps, why does God allow suffering? Using her own very real experiences with suffering from an early age, Keiran explores the reality of suffering and Jesus' response to it. Using His life as an example, she demonstrates the purposes of suffering and how God means for His children to grow as a result of suffering. A must read but especially for anyone experiencing the dark night of the soul."

John J. Sullivan,
ServantLeader Ministries
Author of *Servant First! Leadership for the New Millennium*

"Out of Suffering into Glory" is very beneficial for assisting anyone going through suffering, and helping them find God's redemptive purposes in that suffering. I commend Sally for writing this very relevant and timely work of art, and know it will be a great blessing and comfort. So many helpful insights are scattered throughout this amazing book. It is very appropriate that Chapter 6 is the Center of the book because it is profoundly written and will assuredly be a cold glass of water to anyone thirsting for help through difficult circumstances. I highly recommend this book to you and suggest you purchase one for any loved one going through deep waters.

Rev. Jesse Owens
Pastor, Evangelist, Missionary

If you find yourself wandering in a wilderness of suffering, this is a guide-book home. In this beautifully written book Sally Keiran shares practical insights, thrilling testimonies and profound biblical truths. Whether your hope is to find meaning in what you are facing or a victory amidst the onslaught, Out of Suffering Into Glory is an invaluable tool.

Bill Shuler Senior Pastor
Capital Life Church, Washington DC

It was for the joy of what was set before Him that Jesus journeyed to the cross. Joy and Suffering are something we are all familiar with. In the Kingdom of God, they are sometimes experienced simultane-ously. It has been my privilege to walk, even if in a small way, with Sally

Keiran and her family through both. Her walk has led her to greater compassion for those who live in the open pain of poverty and disease, as well as those who suffer silently under the mask of prosperity and public image. She has learned to mourn with those who mourn and rejoice with those who rejoice. This book invites the reader into her journey. It is one that will leave you, as it has her, with a greater capacity for both compassion and celebration.

Bob Hazlett
Touch of Fire Ministries
Author, Xtreme Christianity

Sally Keiran's book is filled with love for Christ, practical wisdom for all of us who suffer, and profound reminders of God's remedy for all our spiritual ailments. I recommend this loving story heartily and happily!

Bill Jeschke
Pastor of The King's Chapel
Fairfax, Virginia

Everyone suffers but do trials and tribulations, illnesses an accidents make us bitter or better? Sally Keiran's deeply spiritual and timely book is an inspirational work that informs and builds faith for those suffering loss, ongoing medical issues, loneliness, abandonment and other painful issues. No matter how bad things get, God the Father, Son, and Holy Spirit are always near. Sally chronicles the life of Jesus with deep insight and abiding love. Like her Master, she has walked the path of suffering in illness and loss, but in her love and compassion for those who are suffering, she has reached out almost daily to those in need and in doing so she has lived her Master's life for his Glory.

Dr. Alan N. Keiran

Navy Chaplain, Ret. D. Min

Author of *"Take Charge of Your Destiny"* and *"Don't be Surprised"*

"Out of Suffering into Glory" is not only a great title, but something we all have either gone through or are going through, at least the part about suffering. Sally Keiran does a beautiful job of breaking down the concept of suffering. Sally so eloquently points out that Jesus suffered the same way that we do and points the way on how He overcame suffering and that we can do the same. The Bible says in 2 Corinthians 1: 3-4 "Blessed be the God and Father of our Lord Jesus Christ, the Father of mercies and God of all comfort, who comforts us in all our tribulation, that we may be able to comfort those who are in any trouble, with the comfort with which we ourselves are comforted by God." (NKJ)

Sally is a perfect example of one who has endured suffering from the enemy and has turned that suffering into glory by the Power of the Lord Jesus Christ. I highly recommend this book to any person who is going through suffering. Also, Sally relates the vision the Lord has given her concerning the "last days" of God's outpouring of His spirit flowing over the earth, incredible vision.

Rev. Brent Bozarth

Pastor, International Calvary Church

Author of *Shaken and Stirred, but Not Moved*

It has been a blessing to know Mrs. Sally Keiran and it is my great joy to endorse her book, *Out of suffering into Glory*. This book will give great insight, comfort, strength and encouragement to whosoever suffers, for the author does not only understand what suffering means but she has overcome much in her own life journey. Her heart naturally goes out to those who suffer. God has given her His heart for the broken, the lost and the needy. It is not surprising to hear how she has been attracted to the orphans at the Light Children's Home in India and has whole-heartedly ministered not only to these abandoned and suffering kids, but also to widows and lepers in rural India… As Sally declares in her book, God is a Healer! He is able to redeem, restore, and make new our hearts and minds. Through this book, the readers will reach the conclusion that the troubles of life even including death cannot overcome God's love and grace. They simply open new doors to God's glory, if only we stand firm in the Lord. The glory of resurrection is our final destination. For this purpose, God saved us and leads us moment by moment. And for this purpose, in all things, God works for the good of those who love Him and who have been called. This book will inspire every reader to look upon the glory of God in any painful situation and gain real strength to overcome it.

Dr. Sharon Lee
Senior Pastor of International Calvary Church
Springfield, VA

"Sally Keiran's book provides candid and valuable strategies for navigating through seasons of distress and grief. It will bring illumination and comfort to many sufferers. Keiran's remarkable transparency in being willing to draw back the curtain of her personal pilgrimage brings life to this narrative. Her life embodies the principles she shares, modeling in words and actions the path to maximum living. *Out of Suffering Into Glory* has blessed my life."

Rear Admiral Barry C. Black
Chaplain of the United States Senate

Our life is like journeying in the wilderness. There is hardly a way to escape the difficulties and adversities in the wilderness of our life. Even the people of God are not completely free from such difficulties and troubles. On the contrary, the Bible consists of many people who wrestled with their own hardships and problems. God allows His people to take suffering within His divine providence. Sometimes we do not have any idea about God's purpose in our current hardship. However, in the long run, God teaches us His redemptive will in our crises, and makes our faith far more matured and strengthened through them.

This was the case exactly with our Lord. He experienced a great deal of suffering in the world. In God's plan, Jesus' suffering was the way in which God provided human beings with salvation. Furthermore, God exalted Jesus Christ to seat Him at the right hand of His heavenly throne until His second coming. The famous expression, "No cross, no crown," is thus perfect for the case of Jesus' suffering and subsequent glory. I am so pleased to say that Mrs. Sally Keiran's book on Christ's suffering, her own life experiences and her ministry in India surely confirms the biblical truth that God is always with people in their suffering, and He will transform it into the glorious one. Reading this record of the many people of God who experienced great afflictions, I was totally thrilled to see how the Word of God made great impact on those who were suffering, and God took care of them so intimately. I pray that all the readers of this book may be equipped with the most significant testimony of the book — thanks to the sacrifice of our Lord, who entered into our realm *out of glory into suffering*, that we may be brought *out of suffering into glory*. I praise God who transforms our absolute despair into His absolute hope.

Rev. Younghoon LEE, Ph.D.
Senior pastor, Yoido Full Gospel Church
Seoul, Korea

Contents

Preface

For years I wondered why I had to endure much suffering in my childhood. The awareness that life is hard has always been prevalent in my mind. In adulthood I have been drawn to those who suffer and have considered the reasons why suffering occurs. I have sought to remember Job's response when he suffered great tragedy and affliction. "In all this Job did not sin by charging God with wrongdoing" (Job 1:22). There is a mystery to suffering, and many on earth find it easy to accuse God of "doing wrong" when a tragic event occurs or a natural disaster hits. I believe God has allowed many of these thoughts to be in my mind over the years, bringing me to this place of writing a book on suffering.

Also over the past two years I have seen firsthand the suffering of orphans, widows and lepers in India, which has given a face to greater suffering than I ever experienced. I know beyond a shadow of a doubt that God has redemptive purposes in suffering, and He allowed His own Son to come to earth and suffer. In this book I write of the many ways that Jesus suffered while on earth. I want to explain, however, that the themes of the chapters came to me from God. Though I share many ways that Jesus suffered, I do not include every way. I was not led to discuss the suffering Jesus endured in being betrayed by a close friend. Nor did I discuss that He suffered humiliation, weariness, and poverty. Some may consider additional ways He suffered of which I did not write. If you have suffered in ways not discussed in this book, please know that God knows. He cares. And He desires to walk with you through your trials and pain.

Within some of my chapters I used author's discretion to highlight in capital letters or in bold certain attributes of God for emphasis. My desire is that you would have revelation of how incredible God is and recognize His greatness. Also you may find some deliberate repetition between chapters as the subject of forgiveness and foundational truths from God's Word carry over amidst various themes covered.

May God bless you as you read this book and my prayer is that you would come to deeper understanding of God's redemptive purposes for suffering.

Out of Suffering Into Glory!

Chapter 1

Redemptive Suffering

Let us fix our eyes on Jesus,
the author and perfecter of our faith,
who for the joy set before him
endured the cross.
Hebrews 12:2a

Jesus entered our world knowing His life would be one of great suffering. He came for love's sake - *out of glory into suffering* to bring us *out of suffering into glory*. He knows you intimately and loves you beyond measure. He knows your struggles, your weaknesses, and all that you have suffered. He desires to have you open your heart to Him fully to allow Him to walk with you through every season, every storm of your life. He wants to be the Sun which shines brightly even in the midst of the darkness and clouds that touch your life. He wants you to believe in the rainbow of promise you'll discover beyond your present storms. But especially He wants you to know with certainty that He is the one who brings redemptive purpose out of suffering and that you are not alone in your suffering.

I have just returned from our second mission trip ministering to lepers, orphans and widows in Southeast India. They teach me so much — patient endurance, longsuffering, acceptance of what life brings. In our meetings they sit uncomplaining as their faces reflect the deep hunger within for words of encouragement they hope we will bring to them. They are heroes to me. And they suffer much.

In the months prior to this trip, I prayed and asked the Lord what I was to share with my Indian brothers and sisters. He instructed me to share of His sufferings which He experienced while on earth. Not surprisingly His word to me came at a time when I had been experiencing my own suffering in a trial which I endured for much of 2011. It was a very difficult year for me, yet I believed God had His purposes in allowing this, which He will use to bless others. God does not waste our sorrows. He will not waste your sorrows or pain in the economy of His Kingdom. I want you to believe this with all your heart. God loves you and knows your trials and your suffering. He wants you to know Him as the God of Hope. *"May the God of hope fill you with all joy and peace as you trust in him, so that you may overflow with hope by the power of the Holy Spirit"* (Romans 15:13).

As I prepared for our upcoming trip to India in February 2012, and what God wanted me to share in my messages there, I couldn't get out of my mind the men and women I had met in 2010 who have leprosy. Many of them are greatly afflicted by this terrible disease and are missing fingers and toes. As much as they suffer physically, there is also the mental and emotional distress that comes with this disease. In India they are outcasts and are shunned by society and even rejected by family and friends. Most are living in poverty and struggle to survive. I have a hard time envisioning what they suffer. My suffering seems insignificant in comparison to what they endure daily.

Divine Revelation

It was on my birthday the fall of 2011, a day when I was battling to find joy in the midst of my ongoing trial of deep emotional pain and accompanying physical affliction from an undiagnosed source. In my quiet time with the Lord I was led to the Book of Hebrews. Several chapters speak of Christ's suffering and I spent time reflecting on these verses.

In bringing many sons to glory, it was fitting that God, for whom and through whom everything exists, should make the author of their salvation perfect through suffering.

Hebrews 2:10

Therefore, since we have a great high priest who has gone through the heavens, Jesus the Son of God, let us hold firmly to the faith we profess. For we do not have a high priest who is unable to sympathize with our weaknesses, but we have one who has been tempted in every way, just as we are — yet was without sin. Let us then approach the throne of grace with confidence, so that we may receive mercy and find grace to help us in our time of need.

Hebrews 4:14-16

My heart was overwhelmed as I considered the suffering of Jesus. "Lord," I prayed, "how is it You could endure so much while on earth? You went through everything men and women experience in their times of suffering and yet, You did it without sin. You did it for us, to make a way out of our pain, our lostness, our alienation. You loved us so much! You came as a Suffering Servant to show us the way. It is not possible for anyone on earth to say to You, 'You don't know what it's like.' You do know what it is like. You gave up the glory and majesty of heaven to be with mankind in their weaknesses, their selfishness, and their fallenness. Oh what a Savior! How worthy You are to be loved and adored."

During the following week, I was woken at night as the Holy Spirit spoke to me more fully what I was to share in India. In a night of divine revelation God revealed to me the ways Jesus suffered as I considered the suffering of the lepers. Jesus suffered hunger and thirst. He knew grief and rejection. He was in pain, wounded, despised and rejected. He knew anguish and sorrow. And on the cross He was forsaken by His Father and tasted death for mankind. Oh, Jesus!

Have you considered this truth so that you would humbly stand amazed at what our Savior endured ... for you? Love compels one to give sacrificially, and love is the essence of our triune God who suffered for you and me.

The Wonderful Promises of God

Continuing in the night hours reflecting on the suffering of Jesus, I then thought of the wonderful promises He made while proclaiming the Good News of the Kingdom of God. For those who hunger, Jesus declares, *"I am the bread of life. He who comes to me will never go hungry...."* (John 6:35a). For those who thirst, Jesus says, *"If anyone is thirsty, let him come to me and drink. Whoever believes in me, as the Scripture has said, streams of living water will flow from within him"* (John 7:37-38).

Isaiah spoke prophetically of the Messiah that He would understand those who grieve for He was, "*A man of sorrows and acquainted with grief*" (Isaiah 53:3). When his friend Lazarus died, we read in John 11:33-36, "*When Jesus saw her weeping, and the Jews who had come along with her also weeping, he was deeply moved in spirit and troubled. 'Where have you laid him?' he asked. 'Come and see, Lord,' they replied. Jesus wept. Then the Jews said, 'See how he loved him!'*" Jesus understood grief; He saw multitudes who suffered under the curse of death and disease. His compassion for the sorrows of man directed His life in alleviating suffering. And this same God promises that one day, "*He will wipe every tear from their eyes. There will be no more death or mourning or crying or pain, for the old order of things has passed away*" (Revelations 21:4). Jesus is our comforter and the God who will bring us one day into eternal joy.

Jesus lived in the day when many were afflicted with leprosy so He understood those who were unjustly despised, suffering not only physically, but also emotionally. From Isaiah again we read that Jesus Himself, "*was despised and rejected by men*" (Isaiah 53:3). Although multitudes followed Christ during His three years of ministry, many others rejected Him and His teachings, and many still reject Him. To those who feel the pain of rejection Jesus replies, "*If anyone loves me, he will obey my teaching. My Father will love him, and we will come to him and make our home with him*" (John 14:12).

Jesus knows the sorrow of being deserted, for when the hour came that He was arrested in the Garden of Gethsemane, we read in Mark 14:50 concerning His followers, "*everyone deserted him and fled.*" There is great pain in being deserted; Jesus knows that pain and promises that He "*will ask the Father, and he will give you another Counselor to be with you forever — the Spirit of truth. The world* cannot accept him, because it neither sees him nor knows him. But you know him, for he lives with you and will be in you. I will not leave you as orphans; I will come to you" (John 14:16-18). I especially love this promise now that we are involved personally with orphans of the Light Children's Home. The loving kindness of God is revealed by His desire to be with those who are abandoned and alone.

It is difficult to imagine the physical pain Jesus suffered in His crucifixion. He did it for you — He did it for me. *"And they began to call out to him, "Hail, king of the Jews!" Again and again they struck him on the head with a staff and spit on him. Falling on their knees, they paid homage to him. And when they had mocked him, they took off the purple robe and put his own clothes on him. Then they led him out to crucify him"* (Mark 15:18-20). He took the punishment that we deserve because of sin. Love kept Him hanging on the cross that we might escape the wrath which sin warrants. And in His wounding, there is found the power of healing. *"He himself bore our sins in his body on the tree, so that we might die to sins and live for righteousness; by his wounds you have been healed"* (1 Peter 2:24).

The greatest intimacy and fellowship that existed in the universe was severed during Jesus' crucifixion as Jesus experienced the brokenness of His relationship with God His Father. *"And at the ninth hour Jesus cried out in a loud voice, 'Eloi, Eloi, lama sabachthani?' — which means, 'My God, my God, why have you forsaken me?'"* (Mark 15:34) In His abandonment Jesus became the offering for sin whereby the sins of the world were placed on Him. It is in this horrible punishment and anguish that our sins were atoned for, the penalty was paid, and we can know peace again with our Heavenly Father. Oh what a Savior! To us He promises, *"'Never will I leave you; never will I forsake you.' So we say with confidence,*

'The Lord is my helper; I will not be afraid. What can man do to me?'" (Hebrews 13:5b-6).

Because He died, we can live. On the cross, Jesus cried out, *"'It is finished.' With that, he bowed his head and gave up his spirit"* (John 19:30). The greatest promise for eternity we have from Jesus Christ is given to you and to me as we take the step of faith which millions throughout the centuries have taken. *"I am the resurrection and the life. He who believes in me will live, even though he dies; and whoever lives and believes in me will never die. Do you believe this?"* (John 11:25-26) Do you believe there is One who has suffered in every way we have, yet without sin?

The Answer to Every Suffering of Man

In *God Doesn't Waste Your Sorrows,* Paul Billheimer writes,

When God conceived the plan of creation and redemption, He knew of the fall of mankind in advance and accepted the necessary fact of infinite suffering, of suffering Himself the total consequences for the cumulative sin of the world with its resultant sickness, sorrow, suffering, and pain. He knew He could not make a full atonement for sin without actually experiencing in His very own Being the full need of suffering which Eternal Justice would demand for the transgression of universal moral law. He therefore planned to come to earth as man, and it is of the God-man, Jesus, that we are informed:

During the days of Jesus' life on earth, he offered up prayers and petitions with loud cries and tears to the one who could save him

from death, and he was heard because of his reverent submission. Although he was a son, he learned obedience from what he suffered and, once made perfect, he became the source of eternal salvation for all who obey him.[1]

Hebrews 5:7-9

Jesus understands suffering. He knows all that you have suffered in your life and is in Himself the answer to every suffering known to man. He is the fulfillment of all your needs and desires—all the needs of mankind. He is the Bread of Life for the hungry. He is the Living Water for the thirsty. He is the Comforter for those who grieve. The Healer for the sick. The One who comes alongside those who are rejected. He's the Father to the fatherless. The One who will never forsake us. He is the Way, the Truth, and the Life for those who have lost their way. He is the Resurrection and the Life for those facing death. Oh, what a Savior!

God's Word also reveals to us purpose in our suffering. A passage that has been especially meaningful in my life journey speaks of how there can come good out of our troubles.

Praise be to the God and Father of our Lord Jesus Christ, the Father of compassion and the God of all comfort, who comforts us in all our troubles, so that we can comfort those in any trouble with the comfort we ourselves have received from God. For just as the sufferings of Christ flow over into our lives, so also through Christ our comfort overflows. If we are distressed, it is for your comfort and salvation; if we are comforted, it is for your comfort, which produces in you patient endurance of the same sufferings we suffer.

2 Corinthians 1:3-6

In the chapters ahead we'll be looking at Jesus' life on earth, the suffering He endured, and how He redeemed and triumphed over suffering. We'll also look at individuals whose lives will inspire and help us in our own trials and sorrows. My hope is that in looking more closely at the life of Jesus, you will find the strength, encouragement and determination to continue on in your life journey towards the day when *"there will be no more death or mourning or crying or pain, for the old order of things has passed away"* (Revelation 21:4).

From the Father's heart:

My son/my daughter, I know what you are going through. I understand your pain, your sorrow, your trials. I have desired for you to take comfort in knowing that I am walking with you in this time to strengthen you and sustain you. You are not alone. It is my desire to have you discover more of my nature and my heart as you learn to trust me. The tragedies and troubles of this world are common to all mankind. They were never my intention from the beginning of when I created man. It is from sin. And this world is still under the curse. One day this world will know the freedom and release from decay and suffering. It will be a glorious day. Soon it is coming! Trust me, dear one!

Chapter 2

Created To Crave

Then Jesus declared, "I am the bread of life.
He who comes to me will never go hungry,
and he who believes in me will never be thirsty."
John 6:35

Listen, listen to me, and eat what is good,
and your soul will delight in the richest of fare.
Isaiah 55:2b

Pizza? Chinese? Thai? Your neighborhood All U Can Eat Buffet? So many choices for how to satisfy the most common need of man: hunger. I grew up a chubby child with a sweet tooth. My mom died when I was only seven years old after suffering several years with a terminal illness. Out of his grief, my father turned more and more to alcohol and would go out to a local bar, taking my sister and me with him. We would sit in the car with candy bars or Twinkies and comic books waiting for my dad to return. It was a reoccurring activity of my life in those years. I was conditioned from a young age to look to food—especially all the sweet stuff—to satisfy the ongoing emptiness that was present in my life from having no mother and an addicted dad. A lot of pain accompanied those growing up years with an increasing addiction to food and compulsive overeating. The momentary satisfaction of indulging became a substitute for the love and affirmation which my sister and I lacked.

I don't blame my father. He did the best he could, and when he wasn't drinking he was a loving, kind man. He died when I was only twenty-five years old, and before he died there was much forgiveness and restoration in our relationship. Yet, the ongoing food addiction was present in my life for many years, even though I had committed my life to Christ at age twenty.

The Land of Plenty

Many in our nation have an ongoing love affair with food. You may be one of them. It's hard not to. We live in a nation of plenty and if self restrain isn't part of your character makeup, then it is easy to give in to your inner cravings. America is the land of abundance and we see all around us coffee shops, restaurants, and specialty markets with food items to satisfy every craving and desire. Supermarkets and bookstores have all the latest cooking magazines and every imaginable cookbook you'd ever want to own. We live in northern Virginia, an area with one of the highest standards of living in the United States. After traveling on our ministry trips to India in 2010 and 2012, I felt shock in returning home at the ease with which we can overindulge in America. What a contrast to being with our fifty-six sponsored children in the Light Children's Home. Their daily food is primarily rice and dahl (a lentil dish) and occasionally chicken and eggs, which our monthly love gifts help provide.

Several years ago I was reading a book on fasting by Mike Bickle[1] and realized that the lavish lifestyle most of us are accustomed to is a recent development. He said that many westerners have a lifestyle of continual feasting whereas our ancestors from only a generation or two earlier would have had occasional days of feasting on holidays and days of special celebrations throughout the year. Otherwise their daily diet would have been simple and basic. Today however, many feast every day with the rich foods available to us, the ease of eating out, and the ready-made foods in supermarkets that cater to our cravings.

Well, guess what? Craving is God-instilled, according to Lysa TerKeurst, the president of Proverbs 31 Ministries and author of *Made to Crave: Satisfying Your Deepest Desire with God, Not Food.*[2] The author explains that God created us to crave. It is not a bad thing in itself, but it is the longing He put within to crave more of Him. Unfortunately too many look to physical pleasures rather than God to have our deepest needs met. And it is why we continually turn more and more to indulging until we come to understand that God alone will fill that deepest need.

Are you one who needs help in this area? There is much irony in the fact that those in third world countries suffer from actual hunger but many in western nations suffer from guilt, addiction, and serious health problems from too much food. That was my case for many years, overeating from stress, insecurity, emptiness and wrong brain patterns as mentioned earlier. The realization of possible diseases and sicknesses from poor eating choices motivated me to take my health seriously and desire to take care of this temple which God had given me. God was pursuing me and slowly helping me realize my true hunger was for more of Him.

Taste of God's Goodness

What began to transform my life was feeding on God's Word. Jesus declared, *"I am the bread of life. He who comes to me will never go hungry"* (John 6:35). David in Psalm 34:8 states, *"Taste and see that the LORD is good. Oh, the joys of those who take refuge in him!"* As I studied Scripture, I found many verses about hunger including where Jesus Himself hungered after fasting for forty days in His time of temptation in the desert wilderness. This was a time of testing to determine whether He would be obedient to His Father and fulfill God's purpose for His life on earth, or if the temptations of this world would draw Him away from God's plan. If any of you have fasted before, you know the weakness you feel and how your mind can easily be attacked during this time. Our Savior, even in His suffering from hunger, confronted the enemy with the powerful weapon of Scripture.

> *Jesus, full of the Holy Spirit, returned from the Jordan and was led by the Spirit in the desert, where for forty days he was tempted by the devil. He ate nothing during those days, and at the end of them he was hungry. The devil said to him, "If you are the Son of God, tell this stone to become bread." Jesus answered, "It is written: 'Man does not live on bread alone.'"*

> Luke 4:1-4

Jesus wielded the Word to confront His enemy. He did not give in to temptation but showed us the way out. God's Word is powerful and mighty in defeating attacks of the enemy. The Word helped reprogram my early behavior patterns so that I slowly began to lose the weight of my early years. It wasn't any specific diet plan that helped me, but the revelation that God Himself is able to satisfy my inner hunger. (See Appendix for Scriptural Resources.)

King David, who wrote many Psalms throughout his life, beautifully composed the words of Psalm 63 describing the inner hunger of the soul which longs for God.

> *O God, you are my God, earnestly I seek you; my soul thirsts for you, my body longs for you, in a dry and weary land where there is no water... Because your love is better than life, my lips will glorify you. I will praise you as long as I live, and in your name I will lift up my hands. My soul will be satisfied as with the richest of foods; with singing lips my mouth will praise you.*

Psalm 63:1, 3-5

Don't you love those words, *"My soul will be satisfied as with the richest of foods"?* David goes on to unite this declaration with the experience of his life that *"with singing lips my mouth will praise You."* Israel's Shepherd-King discovered that contentment of his soul came when he sang praises to God. *"Because your love is better than life, my lips will glorify you."* Our lips were not only made for communication and eating, but also for praise. A lifestyle of praise has become my source of strength, peace and fulfillment. Praise brings me into the presence of my loving God where my soul finds union with Him. How gratifying it is to use our mouths to offer Him worship and adoration.

The Fruit of Self-Control

God has also revealed to me over the years that He has given us the gift of His Holy Spirit and that an important fruit of the Holy Spirit is self-control. As I meditated on God's word, I realized self-control was not something I could pursue independently of God. I had tried many times in my early years of walking with the Lord to overcome food addiction and overeating. But an experience in my early Christian life of brokenness and surrender to the Lordship of Christ brought me into the baptism of the Holy Spirit according to Acts 1:4-5.

> *On one occasion, while he (Jesus) was eating with them, he gave them this command: "Do not leave Jerusalem, but wait for the gift my Father promised, which you have heard me speak about. For John baptized with water, but in a few days you will be baptized with the Holy Spirit."*

I began to study verses on the Holy Spirit to learn of this incredible gift my Father God had given to me. I saw that at Jesus' baptism the Holy Spirit descended on Him, enabling Him to receive power to fulfill His life mission; so I realized Christians also must be empowered by God's Spirit to enable us to fulfill our destiny our earth. I also discovered that the Holy Spirit brings wonderful fruit into our lives which slowly began to bring inner healing from my painful childhood as I gave God permission to conform me more to the image of Christ. There is a battle that we all encounter, however, between our sin nature and the Spirit, so we have to come to the place of putting to death our old nature with the help of God's Spirit. Out of love and devotion to live for Jesus, we say, "Have your way, God, in my life. Make me more like Jesus."

The apostle Paul dealt with this conflict as he admonished the church in Galatia to overcome wrong cravings with the help of the Holy Spirit.

So I say, live by the Spirit, and you will not gratify the desires of the sinful nature. For the sinful nature desires what is contrary to the Spirit, and the Spirit what is contrary to the sinful nature. They are in conflict with each other, so that you do not do what you want.... But the fruit of the Spirit is love, joy, peace, patience, kindness, goodness, faithfulness, gentleness and self-control. Against such things there is no law. Those who belong to Christ Jesus have crucified the sinful nature with its passions and desires.

Galatians 5:16-17, 22-24

God desires to fill you with His Holy Spirit so that you will have the power to live the Christian life. He also wants you to realize that just as in the natural world fruit can't be produced by itself, so also with spiritual fruit. We cannot produce fruit apart from the vine. Spiritual fruit will be produced by the fullness of the Spirit in your life. Seek to allow God's Spirit to live in you through daily submission and yieldedness of your own life to His will for you. Overcome your sin nature through faith in Christ. His grace will be poured out upon you and you will see fruit result, including the fruit of self-control.

He Fills the Hungry Soul

Jesus declared to His followers the right priorities for life.

I tell you, do not worry about your life, what you will eat; or about your body, what you will wear. Life is more than food, and the body more than clothes. Consider the ravens: They do not sow or reap, they have no storeroom or barn; yet God feeds them. And how much more valuable you are than birds! Who of you by worrying can add a single hour to his life? Since you cannot do this very little thing, why do you worry about the rest? ... So do not set your heart on what you will eat or drink; do not worry about it. For the pagan world runs after all such things, and your Father knows that you need them. But seek his kingdom, and these things will be given to you as well.

Luke 12:22-26, 29-31

Oh, how He loves His children. He knows that we worry. He knows that life today is stressful and the cost of living is continually rising. Life has many challenges including getting food on the table. I think of our sponsored children in India. Their lives have many challenges, but God has heard their prayers for daily provision of food and through our generous donors they now have enough food so they don't have to worry anymore. I have also heard of miraculous provision granted to missionaries in Mozambique who were providing for fifty orphans and had a neighbor give them a casserole dish for their own family of four. That dish was offered to the orphans also, and it ended up feeding fifty-four people, not only four. Wow! Isn't God amazing? (Even the paper plates didn't run out.)

So what is the heart of this matter concerning hunger? Jesus tells you, "I am the Bread of Life, I will not let you go hungry. Seek first a relationship with Me. I will take care of the rest. Know that My Word is Bread for your soul. Feed on it daily. And care for those who are truly hungry. Give to the poor and needy." In one of the most poignant passages of Scripture, Jesus shared, *"For I was hungry and you gave me something to eat, I was thirsty and you gave me something to drink, I was a stranger and you invited me in, I needed clothes and you clothed me, I was sick and you looked after me, I was in prison and you came to visit me…. I tell you the truth, whatever you did for one of the least of these brothers of mine, you did for me"* (Matthew 25:35, 40).

Jesus suffered hunger on earth. He knew physical need, but He also knew that our true hunger is of the soul. That is our deepest longing. He declared in the Beatitudes, *"Blessed are those who hunger and thirst for righteousness, for they will be filled"* (Matthew 5:6). Knowing Jesus <u>will</u> satisfy that God instilled craving and fill us with more than enough.

Pray with me…

O God, You are my God. Help me to seek You with all my heart and help my soul to be as satisfied in my relationship with You as I am enjoying the richest of foods (Psalm 63:1, 5). Jesus, You taught that man does not live by bread alone, but on every Word that comes from Your mouth (Matthew 4:4). I want Your Word to fill me up with spiritual nourishment so I won't keep looking for that which was never meant to satisfy completely. Your kingdom, God, isn't primarily eating and drinking, but it's a kingdom where righteousness, peace and joy abound by Your Holy Spirit. This is what I really desire (Romans 14:17-18). Thank You that You are the Bread of Life. Whoever comes to You will never go hungry, and whoever believes in You will never be thirsty (John 6:35). Take my inner craving and let it find fullness in You alone. Thank you God. Amen!

I will praise you as long as I live…
My soul will be satisfied as with the richest of foods, with singing lips
my mouth will praise you.
Psalm 63:4-5

Chapter 3

Drink Deeply

"If anyone is thirsty, let him come to me and drink. Whoever believes
in me, as the Scripture has said, streams of living water will flow from
within him." By this he meant the Spirit, whom those who believed
in him were later to receive. Up to that time the Spirit had not been
given, since Jesus had not yet been glorified.
John 7:37-39

Another perfect day in Hawaii… Temperature in the eighties,
sunshine, balmy breeze. A great day for a hike in the Pali Mountains
with our kids. Jennifer was home from college for Christmas break,
John was ten years old with lots of energy to expend. All four of us
loved every opportunity to enjoy the beauty of our present duty
station. Hiking in Hawaii was not always as easy as in the main-
land, but we had a map marked with the trails, and we thought
we'd take a short hike before lunch. What we didn't plan ahead for
was water. We assumed it'd be a quick hike in and out, but that's
not how it ended up. We got lost.

The map was not accurate, the trails began to all look alike,
and we had no idea where we were. This had never happened

to us in our many years of hiking. One thing was certain: we were thirsty. Very thirsty! As we continued hiking, my husband and I were giving each other worried looks, not wanting to verbalize our predicament and make our kids panic. But we were getting quite concerned about our lost state and the lack of water. I will admit I had never felt so thirsty in my entire life. We had no certainty of when we would find our way out of the dense mountain wilderness of the Pali Mountains and find water. The consequences of dehydration were beginning to affect us — we felt weak, dizzy and nauseous. I'm sure heat exhaustion was also affecting our bodies. My husband and I each prayed silently so as not to distress our kids, "God help! Save us."

Who Will Quench Your Thirst?

Have you ever been that thirsty? It is not pleasant, is it? As westerners, we are a blessed people with clean, healthy water readily available to us — in our homes, workplaces, stores, and most places of travel. If you have ever been in dire need of having your basic need of water satisfied, you know how desperate you begin to feel, and how nothing else consumes your thoughts except finding water.

God's mercy did eventually lead us out of the mountains. We found our way back to a major trail and back to the parking lot and rest stop area where they had bottled water. Did that water taste good! Nothing on earth would have satisfied in that moment except quenching our thirst.

Have you ever felt that thirsty in your soul? Have you ever been in the position of longing for something to satisfy the empty feeling inside? As a young Christian in the eighties, I loved the praise song "As the Deer" by Martin Nystrom. Based on Psalm 42, the lyrics state,

> *As the deer panteth for the water, so my soul longeth after You. You alone are my heart's desire, and I long to worship You. You alone are my strength, my shield, to You alone may my spirit yield. You alone are my heart's desire, and I long to worship You.*

In His most excruciating time of suffering while on the cross, Jesus cried out, "I thirst!" Already having been through the agony of being beaten, scourged, and nailed to the cross, He cried out, "I thirst!" Was this the heart cry of a Son longing for His Father? Was this cry more than the physical thirst that this innocent Man surely had after all He had been through leading up to the crucifixion? "I thirst." He knew the conditions common to man: of thirst, of longing, of desperation for deliverance from something so deep that only God the Father can satisfy and fulfill.

There was a woman who had a deep soul thirst and tried one relationship after another to fulfill that need. Jesus met with that woman in a divine appointment sovereignly ordained by Father God. In their encounter at a well, which centered around water and thirst, Jesus requested a drink. It was unusual for a man of that time to address an unfamiliar woman, but Jesus knew the woman thirsted for something which only He could offer to her. So He engaged her in conversation.

> *The Samaritan woman said to him, "You are a Jew and I am a Samaritan woman. How can you ask me for a drink?" (For Jews do not associate with Samaritans.) Jesus answered her, "If*

you knew the gift of God and who it is that asks you for a drink, you would have asked him and he would have given you living water." "Sir," the woman said, "you have nothing to draw with and the well is deep. Where can you get this living water? Are you greater than our father Jacob, who gave us the well and drank from it himself, as did also his sons and his flocks and herds?" Jesus answered, "Everyone who drinks this water will be thirsty again, but whoever drinks the water I give him will never thirst. Indeed, the water I give him will become in him a spring of water welling up to eternal life." The woman said to him, "Sir, give me this water so that I won't get thirsty and have to keep coming here to draw water."

John 4:9-15

What would it be like never to thirst again? Could this Man truly be offering something she had never tasted before? Something that would change her life forever? She had a soul thirst which she didn't understand. Jesus knew the innermost need of this Samaritan woman. He knew her many relationships had not brought peace or meaning to her life. In her encounter with the Messiah, she recognized that this Man who offered her "living water" was like no other with whom she had ever spoken. His offer brought hope to the emptiness of her soul, and her eyes were opened to the One who brings salvation and eternal life to the thirsting. Not only was her life changed forever as she recognized the Messiah, but the Scripture tells us that many in her village became believers and declared, "Now we know that this man really is the Savior of the world" (John 4:42).

Streams of Living Water

The imagery of springs is common in the Bible. Isaiah the Old Testament prophet offers beautifully written verses describing God's desire to satisfy the thirst of His people. Some of my favorite passages, which I return to over and over, are those promising refreshment for our soul for times when there is dryness in our lives.

The LORD will guide you always; he will satisfy your needs in a sun-scorched land and will strengthen your frame. You will be like a well-watered garden, like a spring whose waters never fail.

Isaiah 58:11

This is what the LORD says — he who made you, who formed you in the womb, and who will help you: Do not be afraid, O Jacob, my servant ... For I will pour water on the thirsty land, and streams on the dry ground; I will pour out my Spirit on your offspring, and my blessing on your descendants.

Isaiah 44:2-3

My husband Alan and I have a favorite place to visit in Pennsylvania — Boiling Springs. It is a delightful place for a stroll around a spring-fed lake where ducks, geese and swans are in abundance. One of the reasons I find it so refreshing is that the water is so pure. It truly looks life-giving and refreshing. We love nature and scenic beauty, and enjoy hiking by lakes, rivers and streams. Because we ministered in the Navy, we usually would be stationed by the ocean. (Praise the Lord.) But at other times, how disappointing it would be to find bodies of water that were muddied and brown. These would not elicit thoughts of life-giving water. Instead we might ask, "Would anything live by drinking this water?"

Throughout the world the poor suffer from critical shortages of clean drinking water. Children in third world nations die daily from health complications from unsafe water contaminated with bacteria, toxins, and parasites. Reducing waterborne diseases is a major health goal in many developing countries. When we traveled to India in 2010 to visit the Light Children's Home we saw what their drinking water looked like before passing through the purification system. It was brown and muddy in appearance. After passing through the filter, it was clear and pure. How glad we were for dear friends who donated funds to install the purification system for our sponsored children. In simple acts of kindness done in Jesus' name we can dramatically affect the lives of the poor.

The poor and needy search for water, but there is none; their tongues are parched with thirst. But I the LORD will answer them; I, the God of Israel, will not forsake them. I will make rivers flow on barren heights, and springs within the valleys. I will turn the desert into pools of water, and the parched ground into springs.

Isaiah 41:17-18

Thirsting for Meaning

Even as great as the suffering from the actual physical thirst for water is the inner thirst that many suffer (as the Samaritan women did): for love, for significance, for meaningful relationships, for purpose. It is as if they wander in desert wastelands looking for what will quench their inner thirst, but they don't even realize what will truly satisfy their longings. I see it in the faces of youth who wander the malls looking for satisfaction in relationships, looking to spend money on that which won't satisfy, and looking for someplace to belong. I see it in the attitude of people who work on Capitol Hill in Washington DC who wander hallways, thirsting for power, prestige and position to gratify their inner longings. What do you thirst for?

I wonder what thirsty people would pay for true fulfillment. The Psalmist addresses this. *"How priceless is your unfailing love! Both high and low among men find refuge in the shadow of your wings. They feast on the abundance of your house; you give them drink from your river of delights. For with you is the fountain of life; in your light we see light (Psalm 36:6-9).* As I meditated on these words from Scripture, I wrote in my journal what God was speaking to me about His desire to satisfy the thirst of His children.

I am more than enough to satisfy all your needs. Trust that there is a river which will not run dry. There is a Fountain ever flowing that will satisfy the greatest thirst. I know the needs of My people and I say, "Come!" Come to Me and let Me quench your thirst. Come to Me to be refreshed and renewed. Let My water cleanse and wash away all that the world puts on you to mar My image.

I am Living Water that satisfies every soul. I am your Fountain. Stand before Me as you would before the mighty ocean. See in Me the abundance of grace that is available. Stand firm on the Rock looking out at the ocean depths. Keep your eyes on the vastness before you. Look to the horizon and know beyond is more of My glory and riches of grace. Pray for the whole earth to be filled with the knowledge of My glory and to know Me as the Fountain of Life. Drink deeply. Be filled. Trust.

Satisfying thirst is all about Jesus. It is about knowing Him, receiving Him, trusting Him, walking with Him, seeking Him, delighting in Him, believing in Him, listening to Him, fellowshipping with Him, keeping our eyes on Him, desiring Him, loving Him, being satisfied in Him. He is our All in all. He is the Rock upon which we stand. He is the anchor for our souls. He is the Way out of our wilderness. He is our joy, our strength, our peace. His love is unfailing. His grace is sufficient. His mercy never ends. His power is made perfect in weakness.

Water to My Soul

In 2007 God used the imagery of living water to bring me healing from deep pain. My husband and I were at the headquarters for Restoring the Foundation, a Healing Ministry located in North Carolina. I was attending a two-week training session to learn how to do prayer ministry for those suffering from unresolved issues from their past and Alan was writing his first book. During the training the attendees themselves went through healing as we learned the methods we were going to offer others. During one of the sessions I became aware of deep-rooted guilt I carried from my rebellious teenage years. As I've shared earlier, my father had a difficult job raising two girls alone. I treated him very disrespectfully as a disobedient teen. Often my father wouldn't know where I was, what I was doing, or when I was going to return home. These memories came back to me as I sensed God wanting to root something painful out of me that I had held on to for too long. In my room prior to the afternoon session I was listening to a song by Michael W. Smith, "I Can Hear Your Voice."

I'm in the river
That flows from Your throne –
Water of life, water of life
It covers me and I breathe again,
Your love is breath to my soul
I can hear Your voice as You sing over me
It's Your song of hope breathing life into me
I can feel Your touch as I come close to You
And it heals my heart,
You restore and renew

As the song played I began to weep. I remembered the anxiety I caused my father, and my unresolved guilt surfaced. I believed that my sinful lifestyle contributed to my father's continued drinking which led to his early death. But God's desire was to set me free and heal my soul. Through my tears God gave me a vision of my father in heaven with Jesus. He was smiling and looking down at me, and I saw Jesus with His arm around my father. With great love my father said to me, "It's ok now, I forgive you. Everything is fine." Just seeing him smiling, speaking loving words and looking more fully alive than I ever saw him on earth brought healing to my soul. This healing was like water to my soul: cleansing me from guilt, refreshing me, and making me whole.

God is also your healer. He knows the deep pain you carry either from what was done to you or perhaps, as in my case, what you may have done to another. He wants to set you free from this sorrow and pain. As He revealed to me, His love is like a river flowing with healing to restore and make whole. As a plant will wither if it receives no water, many of us are dying from soul-thirst and need His Living Water to bring wholeness to our souls. Read the lyrics again from the song and ask Him to show you any area of your life that He wants to heal. Trust Him. He loves you and is a good Father. I was set free, and God desires all His children to walk in this freedom.

Drink From the Everflowing Fountain

Hudson Taylor was one who understood the truth of the One who heals our deepest hurts and meets all our needs. He was a missionary to China in the 19th century, and he founded the China Inland Mission, which after fifty-one years of ministry included 205 mission stations with over 800 missionaries, and 125,000 Chinese Christians. From the biography, *Hudson Taylor's Spiritual Secret*, we have this marvelous quote:

> *Who does not thirst? Who has not mind-thirsts, heart-thirsts, soul-thirsts or body thirsts.... Jesus can meet all, all, and more than meet.... Can it be? Can the dry and thirsty one not only be refreshed – the parched soil moistened, the arid places cooled – but the land be so saturated that springs well up and streams flow down from it? Even so! And not mere mountain-torrents, full while the rain lasts, then dry again... but, "from within him shall flow rivers" ever flowing, ever deep.*

> *Come and drink, not come and sip, or come and be slightly alleviated. No! We are to be ever coming, ever drinking (constantly, habitually). And no fear of emptying the fountain or exhausting the river![1]*

Six weeks after Hudson Taylor wrote these words in a letter to a friend, he suffered the loss of both his wife and infant son to cholera. Out of sorrow and grieving, he wrote of the promise of his Savior: *"Whoever drinks of the water I give him shall never thirst. (John 4:14) Twenty times a day, perhaps, as I felt the heart-thirst coming back, I cried to Him, "Lord, you promised! You promised me that I should never thirst." How quickly he came and satisfied my sorrowing heart! So much so that I often wondered whether it were possible that my loved ones who had been taken, could be enjoying more of His presence that I was in my lonely chamber."*[2]

God's presence is more than enough to satisfy any thirst. Will you come and drink from the fountain which will never run dry? I have found in thirty-seven years of walking with Jesus that He fulfills all my needs. He satisfies every thirst. I encourage you to accept His offer of Living Water, to run to the River that is always flowing, to spend time in worship, in adoration, in stillness before your God. His Word brings life. Through prayer you can talk with your Father in Heaven, share with Jesus your Savior, invite the Holy Spirit to fill you. Choose to live differently from those in the world, so that you will know the life-giving flow of Living Water that is the wellspring of eternal life.

Pray with me...

Lord, I am often dry and need Your Living Water to satisfy my inner thirst. Please refresh me with Your presence, with the Gift of Your Holy Spirit, so that I will have eternal life. I want to drink from the Fountain which will never run dry. When I find myself in a desert place, help me look to You. This world will not quench my thirst, but spending time with You will bring me wholeness. Thank you for offering Your love in which, above all else, my soul finds peace.

"Come!"
Whoever is thirsty, let him come;
and whoever wishes,
let him take the free gift of the water of life.
Revelation 22:17

ഇ

Chapter 4

A Time For Sorrow, A Time For Joy

You will grieve, but your grief will turn to joy.
John 16:20b

Earth has no sorrow that heaven cannot heal."
Thomas More

The Scriptures tell us that God understands suffering and sorrow. Isaiah the prophet foretold that the Messiah would be "a man of sorrows, and acquainted with grief "(Isaiah 53:3). In His time on earth, Jesus experienced the emotional pain familiar to mankind. He wept, being overcome with sorrow when a beloved friend died. He came upon a funeral procession of a widow grieving for her only son and was moved with compassion. But Jesus did not stop merely at feeling our sadness, He also brought hope to those who grieve. He restored joy to those in sorrow. And He continues to minister today to the hurting. He brings us precious encouragement from His Word. In times of greatest need, He provides caring friends and family. And our Savior promises to walk with us through times of sorrow and suffering.

Familiar verses from the Bible have been a lifeline for centuries for those with sorrowful hearts. *"Weeping may remain for a night, but rejoicing comes in the morning"* (Psalm 30:5b). *"Comfort, comfort my people, says your God"* (Isaiah 40:1). *"I will turn their mourning into gladness; I will give them comfort and joy instead of sorrow"* (Jeremiah 31:13b). God is present with us in our suffering and grief. His Spirit is our comforter and reveals to us the loving arms of God, who carries us when life is so hard that we wonder how we can go on.

I am familiar with grief. I was only seven when I experienced the pain of my mother's death. She had been ill for several years suffering from lupus. My memories of my mom are of my father, my sister Irene, and me visiting her at the hospital in Boston. She would be sitting in a wheelchair, heavily drugged from pain meds. I desperately needed her love and comfort to quiet my fears and insecurity, but she was too ill. I remember my father coming in on an early Sunday morning to tell me the news that my mother was gone and was now in heaven. I didn't really understand, but I knew my father was very sad. It became real as time passed and life became hard. Unhappiness seemed to come upon our family from that point on. The lack of a mother's love created a void for all of us in the family. Yet it would be one of the ways that God's redemptive purposes in suffering would be seen in my life.

Grief touched my life again at age twenty-five when I lost my father from multiple health complications resulting from years of drinking. Sorrow and sadness were frequent companions for many of my early adult years. Perhaps they have been your companions too. Yet, through my walk with Christ I have contended that joy would be my new companion. I have sought to live as a daughter with a loving Heavenly Father who is able to transform by His power and presence the reality of loss and grief into a redeemed reality of joy.

Yet I Will Rejoice in the Lord

A number of years ago I received much encouragement from the powerful little word "yet" which I found in several Scripture passages. Let's look at a verse together. *"Though the fig tree does not blossom and there are no grapes on the vines, though the olive crop fails and the fields produce no food, though there are no sheep in the pen & no cattle in the stalls,* yet *I will rejoice in the LORD, I will be joyful in God my Savior"* (Habakkuk 3:17-19). The writer understood loss, but realized that circumstances do not have to dictate our response to sorrow. With the use of this powerful transition word "yet" there is a pivotal turn that happens between two realities — the physical or material and the spiritual. What will help us overcome sorrow is understanding that the spiritual reality is superior. Sometimes it takes giving voice to a declaration of faith similar to that of the Psalmist that will help us rise above the sorrow we may feel. *"Why are you downcast, O my soul? Why so disturbed within me? Put your hope in God, for I will* yet *praise him, my Savior and my God"* (Psalm 43:5). I can testify that God's love, His presence, the comfort of friends, and the encouragement of the Scriptures have turned my past sorrow into present joy.

When we think about grief we realize that it is about loss, but not only the loss of loved ones. Sorrow and grief can come from many different reasons—loss of health, loss of employment, loss of relationships from estrangement or divorce, loss of a carefree childhood, loss of financial security, loss of dreams, or loss of possessions in a natural disaster. Loss can affect us at various times of life. Our children go off to college and we enter the empty nest. Our parents die and we are now the mature generation for the family. Retirement brings loss of identity for many who have based who they are on what they do. Losses and grief bring us through common stages in our attempt at recovery—denial, anger, bargaining, depression, and acceptance according to Dr. Kubler-Ross. Most people find their way through to acceptance and wholeness, but unfortunately some may get stuck in anger, in sorrow, or in depression for part of their lives. Having a personal relationship with Christ and knowing the promises in His Word can help us in this time and assist us in our return to wholeness and joy.

A Happy-Sad Widow

My mother-in-law Claire has always inspired me as a woman of strong faith. When her husband, Hugh, died in 1980 from Lou Gehrig's disease, I remember being amazed to hear her state that she was a "happy-sad widow." Reflecting on her life she saw that God had blessed them with a good marriage. They had been given enough time after the diagnosis of Hugh's condition to accept the trial that had come into their lives. Gratitude was theirs that Hugh did not have to suffer long and linger as some with this disease. He died less than a year after he became ill. At the end Claire and Hugh enjoyed precious moments of love and appreciation for the blessed life they had shared, with six wonderful children, and strong faith that carried them until the end. Claire's declaration that she was a "happy-sad widow" profoundly touched my heart. I will never forget this declaration of faith and joy rising up even in her time of grief, knowing her God was walking with her in her time of sorrow and would faithfully bring her through. She has remained through her life an optimistic woman of great faith who is dearly loved by all who know her. Jesus' presence sustained her in the midst of her grief and made hope possible.

Throughout His three years of ministry, Jesus' loving heart went out to those who grieved. Early in His ministry He came across a funeral procession. A grieving mother was about to bury her only son.

> As he approached the town gate, a dead person was being carried out — the only son of his mother, and she was a widow. And a large crowd from the town was with her. When the Lord saw her, his heart went out to her and he said, "Don't cry." Then he went up and touched the coffin, and those carrying it stood still. He said, "Young man, I say to you, get up!" The dead man sat up and began to talk, and Jesus gave him back to his mother. They were all filled with awe and praised God. "A great prophet has appeared among us," they said. "God has come to help his people."
>
> Luke 7:12-16

God's glory was revealed as our mighty Savior raised this son from the dead and restored to a grieving mother hope and joy. He is the God of restoration and wants to restore to us joy after our times of sorrow. He is able to lead us out of our times of grief. He understands when we suffer from great loss. No matter what your loss or cause for suffering, He is the God of hope.

One of the touching stories of the Bible involves dear friends of Jesus in their time of grief. Mary and Martha and their brother Lazarus had a special relationship with Jesus. He often stayed at their home in Bethany and enjoyed a close friendship with them. The sisters knew the love that Jesus had for their brother. So when Lazarus became ill and was close to death, they sent word to Jesus. They had faith in Jesus and knew also His power to heal those who were sick. But He did not come right away. He responded to His disciples, *"This sickness will not end in death. No, it is for God's glory so that God's Son may be glorified through it."* (John 11:4).

Jesus stayed where He was for two days. When He arrived in Bethany, He comforted the sisters with His presence. They acknowledged their sorrow as they each came to Him and stated that if only He had been there, Lazarus would not have died, *"When Jesus saw her weeping, and the Jews who had come along with her also weeping, he was deeply moved in spirit and troubled. 'Where have you laid him?' he asked. 'Come and see, Lord,' they replied. Jesus wept. Then the Jews said, 'See how he loved him!'"* (John 11:33-36)

The power of God was revealed in the midst of sorrow and grief as Jesus looked up to Heaven, thanked His Father, and spoke words of authority over death. "Lazarus, come out!" (John 11:43)

Death was overcome as Lazarus was released from the bondage of the grave and restored to life. All those who witnessed this miracle were in utter amazement at seeing the glory of God in the manifestation of the power of life over death. In studying the book of Isaiah we find similar words of power, authority, and promise given by the prophet Isaiah concerning the restoration of Israel. Grab ahold of these words for your life. Let them bring you hope.

> *Say to the captives, "Come out," and to those in darkness, "Be free!" Shout for joy, O heavens; rejoice, O earth; burst into song, O mountains! For the LORD comforts his people and will have compassion on his afflicted ones.*

> Isaiah 49:9,13

Oh how He loves His children. Oh, how He loves you. He knows your sorrows, He knows the losses you have suffered in life and He comforts you with these words:

My child, trust Me. Know My comfort. Know that I walk with you through every trial and time of grief. I will strengthen your heart and bring healing. I will pour out My Spirit of grace and consolation to lift you up above all that weighs you down. Look up to Me. Keep your eyes on Me in your sorrow. I am near your side. I walk with you and will bring you to a place of standing firm once again soon. Trust. The sorrow is for a season, but My joy is ever present to fill your heart with My love. I will never leave you.

Your Grief Will Turn to Joy

As Jesus was approaching the end of His ministry, He prepared His followers by revealing that a time of grief would soon come upon them. He also wanted them to know that joy would be theirs as well. His heart was always filled with compassion. In the days ahead they would see their beloved Lord scourged and crucified. Out of concern, He shared words of encouragement with them, directing their hearts towards joy that would replace the sorrow they would soon experience.

> *I tell you the truth, you will weep and mourn while the world rejoices. You will grieve, but your grief will turn to joy.... Now is your time of grief, but I will see you again and you will rejoice, and no one will take away your joy.*
>
> John 16:19b-20, 22

There is another way that grief comes into our lives. Besides grief from losses, the apostle Peter shares in his letter to the early church of grief that comes from our trials.

> *In this you greatly rejoice, though now for a little while you may have had to suffer grief in all kinds of trials. These have come so that your faith – of greater worth than gold, which perishes even though refined by fire – may be proved genuine and may result in praise, glory and honor when Jesus Christ is revealed. Though you have not seen him, you love him; and even though you do not see him now, you believe in him and are filled with an inexpressible and glorious joy...*
>
> 1 Peter 1:6-8

In my many years of walking with the Lord I have read these words over and over and over again. This is one of the passages I memorized early in my Christian life for the encouragement it gives that there is a Heavenly purpose in our trials. Do you truly understand that your faith is of greater worth to God than gold? No matter what your trial or suffering, your faith is tested and proved genuine in the midst of walking through every storm or fiery ordeal in your life. I understand — and I've been there in times when we wonder how we will get through this. But God is faithful! He will not abandon you. He will walk beside you, and carry you through until you are strong enough to stand on your own again. God declares to you that He will *"comfort all who mourn, and provide for those who grieve – to bestow on them a crown of beauty instead of ashes, the oil of gladness instead of mourning, and a garment of praise instead of a spirit of despair"* (Isaiah 61:2-3).

One of the most moving testimonies I've heard recently involves a pastor from New Hampshire whose daughter was killed by a drunk driver. After a time of grieving Pastor Smith (all names have been changed to protect identity) felt God urging him to go to the prison where the young man who killed his daughter was serving his sentence. He knew that as a Christian we are called to forgive others for their offenses against us. In prayerful obedience this grieving father visited Carl and shared that by God's grace he forgave him for causing the accident which led to the loss of his daughter's life. Carl's heart was touched by this act of kindness. An ongoing relationship began with Pastor Smith visiting Carl monthly. He became hungry for God's love and soon prayed to receive the free gift of salvation through Jesus Christ. God's amazing mercy and unconditional love led to the deepening of their relationship and Pastor Smith became like a father to Carl. When his time was served, Carl remained in the area and continues to be a part of Pastor Smith's family. God has brought joy where there had been grief. *Out of Suffering Into Glory!*

I believe there is rejoicing in heaven and God is glorified when Christians reflect grace in trials and prove faith to be authentic. Forgiveness, mercy, and compassion lessen the effect of our losses and suffering and reveal the image of Christ to which we are being conformed. The importance of forgiveness cannot be stressed enough as our Savior Himself often spoke of the need to forgive. It can be one of the keys to releasing you from the grief and pain of your trials, whereas bitterness and unforgiveness can imprison you and keep you from healing. Listen to these vital truths from God's Word.

For if you forgive men when they sin against you, your heavenly Father will also forgive you. But if you do not forgive men their sins, your Father will not forgive your sins.

Matthew 6:14-15

And when you stand praying, if you hold anything against anyone, forgive him, so that your Father in heaven may forgive you your sins.

Mark 11:25

And do not grieve the Holy Spirit of God, with whom you were sealed for the day of redemption. Get rid of all bitterness, rage and anger, brawling and slander, along with every form of malice. Be kind and compassionate to one another, forgiving each other, just as in Christ God forgave you.

Ephesians 4:30-32

Who do you forgive? Parents, siblings, spouses, teachers, bullies, co-workers, strangers, yourself, and anyone who has caused us grief in bringing trials and suffering into our lives. God will bring to you the face and name of the one to whom He wants you to extend grace. Do it for Jesus' sake, because as he hung on the cross, He said, "*Father forgive them, for they know not what they are doing*" (Luke 23:34). The greatest offense ever committed against an innocent man was forgiven by the Author of Grace. Jesus makes that grace available to you to forgive anything that has brought you grief or suffering. Would you receive that grace right now?

Pray with me...

Father, I need to be honest. There are hurts hidden away in my heart that still cause me pain. I have not allowed myself to grieve completely in my desperate need to appear ok. Losses, trials, and offenses have caused wounds which need to be healed. Would You help me heal—by Your grace? Would You help me forgive—by Your grace? Help me to believe that nothing is impossible for You and that You can assist me in rooting out bitterness and resentment hidden within. I <u>will</u> forgive those who have caused me grief. I <u>will</u> trust You. I <u>do</u> believe Your grace is sufficient. Your love for me is so great and Your desire is to bring me joy instead of sorrow. You have given me this wonderful promise, and for this future hope I thank you. Amen.

Now the dwelling of God is with men,
and he will live with them.
They will be his people, and God himself
will be with them and be their God.
He will wipe every tear from their eyes.
There will be no more death or mourning
or crying or pain,
for the old order of things has passed away.

Revelations 21:3-4

Chapter 5

Rejected By Man, Embraced By God

He was despised and rejected by men.
Isaiah 53:3

It is springtime; the renewal of the earth is exploding in brilliant colors around us. As I write this, holy week has just passed with the joy of celebrating the resurrection of Jesus Christ from the dead and with the somber reflection on the suffering of the precious Lamb of God. You may be like many who anticipate the joy of celebrating Easter but haven't stopped to consider what Jesus really went through prior to His death.

In the Triumphal Entry of Jesus into Jerusalem for Passover, we read of the glory and honor that the crowds bestowed on Jesus as He entered Jerusalem riding on a colt. The whole city was stirred and the people, waving palm branches, could not hold back exuberant praise of the man they saw as their Savior-King.

When He came near the place where the road goes down the Mount of Olives, the whole crowd of disciples began joyfully to praise God in loud voices for all the miracles they had seen: "Blessed is the king who comes in the name of the Lord!" "Peace in heaven and glory in the highest!"

Luke 19:37-38

How is it possible that human nature can so easily turn from praise to rejection? This same crowd gathering for the Passover was chanting "Crucify him!" only days later. Perhaps you have seen this in your own life. You have received words of love, affirmation, and sentiments of praise, which in time turn into criticism and rejection. Oh, the unpredictability of man. Jesus understood what was in the heart of man, and stated that He would not accept praise from men (John 5:41). Rather, He declared, *"I seek not to please myself but Him who sent me"* (John 5:30b). The heart of man cannot be trusted because of sin nature. We witness the fickleness of the crowds who were ready to make Him their King but in a few short days rejected Jesus and called for the crucifixion of the Son of Man.

Jesus knew rejection would come. He had warned His followers of what lay ahead for Him in Jerusalem. As a Jew, Jesus was familiar with the words of the prophet Isaiah, that the suffering servant would be despised and rejected (Isaiah 53:3). Concerned for His disciples, He prepared them for what they would soon witness in the fulfillment of God's plans for the redemption of mankind in the sacrifice of the sinless Lamb of God. We read in the Gospel of Mark, *"He then began to teach them that the Son of Man must suffer many things and be rejected by the elders, chief priests and teachers of the law, and that he must be killed and after three days rise again. He spoke plainly about this"* (Mark 8:31-32a).

His Open Arms—the Open Door

There is a deep painful suffering in rejection that comes from being refused, shunned, or denied. The emotional sting of not being accepted can affect you for years or even a lifetime. Playmates, siblings, parents may reject us. Colleges, employers, dating partners may turn us away. We all suffer from rejection at some time. You may be presently experiencing the pain of rejection, which might be interfering with the quality of your life today. Be encouraged. There is one who felt every sting you felt, who speaks tenderly to you even now...

I will not turn you away. Come to Me. My arms are open wide to you. Run to Me, let Me embrace you. I will heal the pain in your heart and affirm My love for you. I will receive you to Myself in intimate relationship and never cast you away. Trust. Listen to My voice.

As I reflected on Holy Week just passed, I thought of all that Jesus went through for us. He was despised, rejected, scorned, misunderstood, insulted, and renounced. In the garden of Gethsemane the weight of the sins of the world soon to be placed on Him caused such anguish that Jesus said to His disciples, "*My soul is overwhelmed with sorrow to the point of death. Stay here and keep watch with me*" (Matthew 26:38). We will be looking at His further suffering in the chapters ahead, but as we stay on the theme of rejection here, we see even on the cross this particular suffering He endured for us.

Those who passed by hurled insults at him, shaking their heads and saying, "You who are going to destroy the temple and build it in three days, save yourself! Come down from the cross, if you

are the Son of God!" In the same way the chief priests, the teach-
ers of the law and the elders mocked him. "He saved others," they
said, "but he can't save himself! He's the King of Israel! Let him
come down now from the cross, and we will believe in him. He
trusts in God. Let God rescue him now if he wants him, for he
said, 'I am the Son of God.'" In the same way the robbers who
were crucified with him also heaped insults on him.

Matthew 27:39-44

All this pain, suffering, and rejection He experienced for us to
pay the penalty for our sin. He endured great agony, taking upon
Himself the punishment for sin by becoming the sin offering. He
was the perfect sacrifice that would take away the sins of the world.
He opened the way to Heaven and, as Scripture tells us, in the
moment of His death, "... *when Jesus had cried out again in a loud*
voice, he gave up his spirit. At that moment the curtain of the temple was
torn in two from top to bottom" (Matthew 27:50-51). The way was
opened into the Holy of Holies, into the presence of God Almighty.
No longer is there a separation between man and God. From this
point on all who call on the Name of the Lord, will be saved.

This is the power of the Gospel and the Good News for the
world. It is also a message that requires a response. What do we
do with this man Jesus? Is He just a good teacher, one who showed
mankind the right way to live? Or is He the Savior, who came to
reconcile us to Father God and open the way to Heaven? If He is
the Savior of the world, He is speaking words of love to you and to
me, "Come!"

I see Him standing before an open door as crowds pass by. He is
looking at each one with eyes of deep compassion and a desire for

relationship. He is pointing out, "Here is the Way. Walk this way. Come! Here is what you are looking for." However, the crowds continue on the way they have chosen, I see them walking by the open door, rejecting Jesus' offer. He paid a terrible price to open that door into the Kingdom of Heaven and many continue to reject our Savior God. My heart is grieved as I think of Jesus' great suffering and the pain of rejection He continues to face in our world. The door is only open for a time and then it will be shut.

> *Enter through the narrow gate. For wide is the gate and broad is the road that leads to destruction, and many enter through it. But small is the gate and narrow the road that leads to life, and only a few find it.*

> Matthew 7:13-14

> *Then Jesus went through the towns and villages, teaching as he made his way to Jerusalem. Someone asked him, "Lord, are only a few people going to be saved?" He said to them, "Make every effort to enter through the narrow door, because many, I tell you, will try to enter and will not be able to. Once the owner of the house gets up and closes the door, you will stand outside knocking and pleading, 'Sir, open the door for us.' But he will answer, 'I don't know you or where you come from.'"*

> Luke 13:22-25

Today we continue to live in the time when the door is open. There is still the invitation to come to Christ; for those who have suffered the pain of rejection, Jesus offers the joy of acceptance. The greatest experience of my life was coming to Christ in 1974 and having His joy overcome years of pain and sorrow. What great delight it is to know that I am accepted in Christ, and loved by Christ, and that by grace through faith, there is nothing I can do that would cause Him to turn me away or reject me. I am His and He is mine forever. You can experience this joy as well. You can receive salvation and forgiveness from all your sins, and become a child of God, a member of the Body of Christ, a part of the Kingdom of God, and receive the abiding presence of God's Holy Spirit. (See Luke 11:13.) This is His promise, "*Yet to all who received him, to those who believed in his name, he gave the right to become children of God*" (John 1:12). In addition, we have this incredible assurance from Romans 5:17 (the Message version), "*If death got the upper hand through one man's wrongdoing, can you imagine the breathtaking recovery life makes, sovereign life, in those who grasp with both hands this wildly extravagant life-gift, this grand setting-everything-right, that the one man Jesus Christ provides?*"

Blessed Are You When Men Hate You

This is Good News worth pursuing. It is the power that changed our world. The message of Jesus' life, death, resurrection, and salvation by faith in Christ was in the hearts of a small group of Jesus' followers who waited in an upper room after His ascension into heaven for the promise of the Holy Spirit. The Spirit came upon 120 followers in that room with power and boldness, and out they went into the streets of Jerusalem. Peter addressed the crowd with the first sermon of the Christian faith.

Therefore let all Israel be assured of this: God has made this

Jesus, whom you crucified, both Lord and Christ." When the people heard this, they were cut to the heart and said to Peter and the other apostles, "Brothers, what shall we do?" Peter replied, "Repent and be baptized, every one of you, in the name of Jesus Christ for the forgiveness of your sins. And you will receive the gift of the Holy Spirit. The promise is for you and your children and for all who are far off – for all whom the Lord our God will call.

Acts 2:36-39

Three thousand were added to the church that day and another five thousand a few days later. Today we have over two billion followers of Christ around the world. These have come out of various backgrounds, many coming to faith in the midst of nations where Christians are a minority and followers of Christ suffer persecution and much rejection. They are committed to stand firm in faith even under such difficult circumstances.

These are the ones who understand, along with their Savior, the suffering that comes from being rejected, scorned, shunned, even outcasts. On our last visit to India, our brothers there told us again how they are not treated the same as non-Christians in business, in employment, in government, and in education. They suffer rejection regularly in living as Christ followers in a non-Christian country. Severe persecution affects Christians in close to fifty countries worldwide.

The apostle Peter wrote about persecution in his letter to the early church. He encouraged believers that from suffering would come joy and revelation of the glory of God.

Dear friends, do not be surprised at the painful trial you are suffering, as though something strange were happening to you. But rejoice that you participate in the sufferings of Christ, so that you may be overjoyed when his glory is revealed. If you are insulted because of the name of Christ, you are blessed, for the Spirit of glory and of God rests on you. If you suffer, it should not be as a murderer or thief or any other kind of criminal, or even as a meddler. However, if you suffer as a Christian, do not be ashamed, but praise God that you bear that name.

1 Peter 4:12-16, 17

God reveals that He will bless those who are insulted and rejected for His sake. As Peter encouraged, "the Spirit of glory and of God rests on you." The Message version of v. 14 states it this way, "If you're abused because of Christ, count yourself fortunate. It's the Spirit of God and his glory in you that brought you to the notice of others." You are different because of Christ in you. His Spirit resides in you, His glory surrounds you, and it is noticed by the world. You are not alone in your suffering and in the rejection which at times you suffer for Christ. Christ suffered, and His words have encouraged Christians throughout the centuries. Rejoice that you are counted worthy of bearing His name.

Blessed are you when men hate you, when they exclude you and insult you and reject your name as evil, because of the Son of Man. Rejoice in that day and leap for joy, because great is your reward in heaven. For that is how their fathers treated the prophets.

Luke 6:22-23

Father, Forgive Them

For some Christians the rejection and persecution may come daily as they live with an unbelieving spouse or unkind co-worker. I know a number of people who endure much for the sake of Christ by remaining in a marriage to a spouse who does not follow Christ. Suffering in the workplace is not uncommon either and made even more grueling because these people are seen every day. There is much pain and hardship in these interactions, but there is also help. Fix your eyes on Jesus, receive His unconditional love. In the trials of life, followers of Christ are given the privilege of learning to love like Jesus — to open their hearts to the fountain of His love which never runs dry. Is this possible? Can you live a life of victory while living day to day in an atmosphere of rejection and emotional pain?

First, recognize and truly understand the truth that Jesus alone fills your deepest needs. To His followers Jesus stated, *"If anyone loves me, he will obey my teaching. My Father will love him, and we will come to him and make our home with him" (John 14:23).* You are indwelt by the Spirit of God if you have received Jesus into your life as Savior and Lord. God has come to live with you through spiritual rebirth. Through that relationship you have God's acceptance and affirmation of your worth, no matter what others think of you. Francis of Assisi once stated, ""Blessed is the man who thinks no better or worse of himself when he is scorned and despised by men than when he is loved and honored by them. For a man is what he is in God's eyes and no more."

Also through the intimacy you have with Jesus, you have access to His joy each day, moment by moment. A wonderful

Old Testament promise states that, "the joy of the Lord is your strength" (Nehemiah 8:10). Joy can rule in your heart regardless of fiery darts or stinging arrows thrown at you because you are loved by the Lord and His arms are always open to you. I often find great joy and peace in these loving words of the Father, *"Let the beloved of the Lord rest secure in him, for He shields him all day long, and the one the Lord loves rests between his shoulders"* (Deuteronomy 33:12).

Second, to receive the blessings of a relationship with Christ, you must forgive the hurts and offenses that come to you by unthinking people. How many times must you forgive? One of Jesus' disciples thought perhaps seven times would be enough, but Jesus said seventy-seven (Matthew 18:21-22). Meaning you forgive as many times as you must. Remember, Jesus also went through suffering and rejection. *"But first he must suffer many things and be rejected by this generation"* (Luke 17:25). What was Jesus' response as He endured this pain? *"Forgive them Father, for they know not what they are doing"* (Luke 23:34). This verse was mentioned in the previous chapter, and it is worth looking at again. I must confess that there are many, many times I have had to repeat these words when I have felt rejected and hurt. Somehow it helps to declare, *"they know not what they are doing."* If they had God's heart of love and His Spirit, they would not act in hurtful ways. They would have wisdom and understanding enabling them to treat others as they themselves would want to be treated.

I have also found that sometimes we have to cry out to God for His love for difficult people. God's love is known as Agape (one of the Greek words for love), and it is the unconditional, sacrificial love of God that reflects the essence of His nature. It's love that gives understanding, kindness, compassion, and forgiveness even when the other does not love or respond back in kind. Our human love will always be deficient in oppressive situations. But God's love *"keeps no record of wrongs"* (1 Corinthians 13:5) and *"covers a multitude of sins"* (1 Peter 4:8). Some of you may have suffered terrible pain from rejection. Yet, to continually allow it a major place in your thoughts and memories only hurts yourself. Sylvia Gunter gives this advice to those who have been offended, "We may think we need our offenders to say, 'I am sorry. Please forgive me.' We do not need the injustice avenged or an apology as much as we need God and what He will give us. Far more than what they could give us with 'I'm sorry,' God would say to us, 'You don't need an apology You need Me. Put yourself in My bosom, the place of healing and freedom. I am your very great Reward.'"[1] Christ came to free us from strongholds and un-forgiveness. We have His grace and His Agape love available to help us release others from our imposed prisons so that they also may experience the forgiveness and love of Christ the Savior.

Out of Suffering Into Glory! Brothers and sisters, here are some final thoughts. I know some of you need to follow the apostle Paul's admonition as I have had to through much of my life. *"One thing I do: Forgetting what is behind and straining toward what is ahead, I press on toward the goal to win the prize for which God has called me heavenward in Christ Jesus"* (Philippians 3:13-14). Once the work of forgiveness is done, you can move past the pain and suffering and pursue the glory of what is coming as Christ's redemptive purposes are seen even in suffering rejection. Look to Jesus. Receive His embrace. Rejoice in Him always. *"Give thanks in all circumstances, for this is God's will for you in Christ Jesus"* (1 Thessalonians 5:18).

Pray with me...

Jesus, with Your help I will look at Your example and move beyond the pain of rejection. I know that Your love for me is unconditional and You will never reject me as my heart is turned to You in faith and commitment. Thank You for Your Word telling me that Your blessings come to those who are persecuted, insulted or rejected. I want to fix my eyes on You, release others from unforgiveness, and look forward to my reward in heaven. I trust You to use my pain for good as I allow myself to know the joy of Your loving arms embracing me. I am secure in You, I am shielded and at peace in You. Amen!

Blessed are you when men hate you,
when they exclude you and insult you
and reject your name as evil,
because of the Son of Man.
Rejoice in that day and leap for joy,
because great is your reward in heaven.
Luke 6:22-23

Chapter 6

Trust: God's Antidote
For A Troubled Heart

You will keep in perfect peace
him whose mind is steadfast,
because he trusts in you. Trust in the LORD forever,
for the LORD, the LORD, is the Rock eternal.
Isaiah 26:3-4

The powerful images of the deadly tsunami coming ashore in Sendai region of Japan are forever etched in my memory. Watching the television on March 11, 2011 at the devastation coming upon the nation of the Rising Sun flooded me with alarm for a people dear to my heart. Our son John is from Japan. We were stationed with the Marines in Iwakuni, Japan from 1986-89 and adopted our son there. People around the world could only pray in those first days of unbelievable suffering coming upon the victims of this catastrophe.

Earthquakes, hurricanes, tornadoes, and other natural disasters cause material devastation and emotional distress for those affected. Fear, anxiety, shock, worry, disturbed sleep, and other emotions afflict the individual who has suffered a traumatic event. But it is not only the fury of nature that brings distress and emotional suffering into our lives, but also the everyday troubles of our human existence that touch our lives and rob them of peace and contentment.

No one is immune from the heartaches of life. Suffering comes in many ways — to good and bad, rich and poor, young and old. King David describes a time of great emotional distress that came upon him as he faced enemies seeking to destroy him. David is known in Scripture as a worshipper who loved to enthusiastically express praise to his God. His writings, found in the Old Testament, reflect great emotions that lead from suffering into acknowledgement of the God in whom he trusted. Listen to his emotional plea.

> *The waves of death overwhelmed me; floods of destruction swept over me. The grave wrapped its ropes around me; death laid a trap in my path. But in my distress I cried out to the Lord; yes, I cried to my God for help. He heard me from his sanctuary; my cry reached his ears.... He reached down from heaven and rescued me; he drew me out of deep waters. He rescued me from my powerful enemies, from those who hated me and were too strong for me. They attacked me at a moment when I was in distress, but the Lord supported me. He led me to a place of safety; he rescued me because he delights in me.*
>
> 2 Samuel 22:5-7; 17-20

God as our compassionate Creator sees all that befalls mankind. He knows the stress, fear, worry, and anxiety that follow us in our day-to-day living. Psalm 34 tells us, *"A righteous man may have many troubles...*" (Psalm 34:19). Well, that doesn't surprise you does it? Yet somehow we think in living a good life we'd be immune from some of these troubles. Again the Psalmist expresses, "*...troubles without number surround me*" (Psalm 40:12). I know that whenever troubles come upon me, it is my chance to see God move on my behalf. We are not alone in this world. There is a God who see and cares about what happens to His children. Let your hearts respond as David did, "*Be pleased, O Lord, to save me; O Lord, come quickly to help me.... You are my help and my deliverer*" (Psalm 40:13, 17).

In my early years after my mom died, I knew many hardships, experienced much fear and had to battle worry. Many of the events from my childhood caused emotional distress to lodge in my heart and contribute to ongoing pain in my adult years. Here is one memory in particular:

The snow was falling heavily in the ongoing storm, my sister and I continually looked out the window into the dark night, asking in our hearts an ever-familiar question, "When will daddy come home?" Anxiety continued to pound in our chests as we waited for the sound of his truck bringing him home from another snow plowing job. We were alone in the house, it was cold, and the wind blew through the old windowpanes. We tried to distract ourselves with play, but it was difficult in such a bad storm to find peace within. "When will daddy come home?"

Fear and darkness were familiar to my sister and me. Our father loved us and tried his best, yet worry had settled into his soul as he raised his girls as a widower. Situations bordering on neglect and a sense of abandonment were a part of our lives. In most cases emotional distress is passed on to the next generation when there has been trauma and dysfunction in a family. Yet, our gracious and kind Savior can take the suffering, the distress, and the anxiety of our past and use it for good in His Kingdom. I have counseled many over the past thirty years who have also had fear, anxiety, and stress from childhood events, which try to rob them of present peace as adults. But our God is a Healer! He is able to redeem, restore, and make our hearts and minds new as we put our trust in Him. He did it in my heart and is able to do it in yours. I am not totally healed from emotional pain, but I have come to discover the key to emotional health is found in having a personal relationship with Jesus. He has been with me for thirty-seven years in good times and bad. He has revealed His love for me over, and over, and His Word is living in my heart to strengthen me when any new trial or distress comes into my life.

Jesus' Surrender—Our Answer

Let's continue to reflect on the life of Jesus, looking especially at His suffering, recognizing that He shared in the humanity of those He came to save in experiencing all that we experience. We come to the time when Jesus fought His greatest battle while praying in the Garden of Gethsemane. Here He faced his supreme temptation. Would He follow the course marked out for Him by His Father in becoming the perfect sacrifice for sin, or would He choose another way? In Gethsemane Jesus knew anguish like no one had ever experienced. Can any of us ever fully comprehend the turmoil, the sorrow, and the brokenness of His heart as He anticipated the weight of the sins of mankind coming upon Him who knew no sin?

*Then Jesus went with his disciples to a place called Gethsemane, and he said to them, "Sit here while I go over there and pray." He took Peter and the two sons of Zebedee along with him, and he began to be **sorrowful and troubled**. Then he said to them, "My soul is **overwhelmed with sorrow** to the point of death. Stay here and keep watch with me." Going a little farther, he fell with his face to the ground and prayed, "My Father, if it is possible, may this cup be taken from me. Yet not as I will, but as you will."*

Matthew 26:36-38

From the other Gospel passages, which describe this excruciating time in Jesus' life, we have Mark share that, *"He began to be **deeply distressed and troubled**."* (Mark 14:33) Luke's Gospel portrayal of the Son of God includes, *"An angel from heaven appeared to him and strengthened him. And **being in anguish**, he prayed more earnestly, and his sweat was like drops of blood falling to the ground"* (Luke 22:43-44). Oh Jesus, what a Savior! It was not just the fearful expectation of crucifixion that caused such agony of His soul. It was the knowledge that soon the terrible wrath of God against sin and iniquity would be placed on Him. In fulfillment of Isaiah's prophecy, we see God's plan of redemption. *"We all, like sheep, have gone astray, each of us has turned to his own way; and the LORD has laid on him the iniquity of us all.... For he was cut off from the land of the living; for the transgression of my people he was stricken"* (Isaiah 53:6, 8b).

It is important that we understand that in the Biblical theology of the Jewish sacrificial system, the means to atone for or pay the penalty for sin was in taking the life of a lamb whose blood would redeem man from sin. The lamb without blemish would be brought to the altar and slaughtered. As the priest laid his hands on the sin offering and confessed the sins of the people, the lamb would symbolically take into itself the sins and guilt of the transgressors.

For Christ, praying in the Garden of Gethsemane, the decision to become the sin offering was not easy. Though the heart of Christ was filled with love for mankind, He wrestled as a human with obeying the will of God. *"My Father, if it is possible, may this cup be taken from me"* (Matthew 26:38). It wasn't just the physical pain of death on a cross He dreaded, but having the guilt of murderers, thieves, liars, molesters, idolaters, and prideful sinners placed on Himself. You probably have seen the various versions of the life of Christ as portrayed in movies. These do not do justice to what our Savior suffered. He called for His closest followers to be with Him in this time of sorrow and pray with Him. They could not and were found sleeping as Jesus, alone in His suffering, wrestled with His choice.

In the selfless surrender of Jesus' will to His Father's, we have been redeemed and set free from the curse of sin and death. Jesus' ultimate battle against Satan in Gethsemane resulted in the most costly declaration ever made on earth: *"Yet not as I will, but as you will."* (Matthew 26:36-38) The cost was His life. And His blood brought forgiveness for all the sins of the world ever committed, or ever to be committed, to those who repent and receive by faith the free gift of salvation. In His surrender, Jesus revealed His complete trust in His Father, to whom He would be restored, though He would suffer the pain of the Father's face turning away from Him.

Hide God's Word in Your Heart

Jesus knows what you have suffered in the past and what you are suffering in your present trial. Jesus endured painful separation from God for us, so that we don't ever have to face a choice like He did. We can go to Him with our fears and worries, and He will lift them from us as we trust Him. He fought the battle with fear for you and for me. He knows how easy it is to worry, to have anxiety and fear come against you to steal your peace and trust. There is an antidote. It is in Jesus. He is the answer to all life's stresses, fears, and worries. He is faithful and we can trust Him in all of life. Let's understand this more fully as we look at God's Word.

In this world you will have trouble. But take heart! I have overcome the world.

John 16:33b

Do not let your hearts be troubled. Trust in God; trust also in me.

John 14:1

Anxious thoughts may fill my heart, but your presence is my joy and consolation.

Psalm 94:19

How to Overcome

Because we have a Savior who has suffered in life as we do but has overcome, we can look to His example in how to become stronger and glorify God through our troubles. Anxiety, worry, and fear do not have to rule over us; we can win the battle in our minds and learn to trust God. Think about the life of Jesus. One thing we see in His life was that He was a man of prayer who rose early to spend time in fellowship with His Heavenly Father. In these hours He spent communing with God, I believe His spirit was strengthened, revelation was received, guidance was given, and comfort and peace were released into His heart. If our Savior needed this time in prayer, how much more do we need to spend time waiting and seeking God at the beginning of each day? My husband and I in over thirty years of ministry have found this early morning quiet time in God's presence invaluable in keeping our hearts peaceful and trusting that He is the Blessed Controller of all things. At the end of the day we also pray together and ask God to protect us, watch over our loved ones, and bring souls into His Kingdom, and then we offer Him our love and adoration as we go to sleep.

One of the most important things you can do to maintain your trust in God is to read, meditate on and memorize God's Word. Scripture is living and powerful (Hebrews 4:12). It will keep you from being overcome by the stresses, worries, and troubles of life. Again we have encouragement from King David who declared, *"When I am afraid, I will trust in you. In God, whose word I praise, in God I trust; I will not be afraid. What can mortal man do to me?"* (Psalm 56:3-4) In practical terms I will share that at times when my emotions are getting the best of me, and my mind is filled with anxious thoughts, I pick up my Bible and know God will bring me peace and strengthen me through what I read. I love God's Word. I love memorizing verses—hiding them in my heart for when I need God's powerful weapon against an attack from the enemy of my soul. Many times I use my concordance and find verses on a theme like trust or peace or grace and then declare these verses out loud which builds up my spirit. (See Appendix for Thematic Verses.)

So many verses have been an anchor for my soul through the everyday struggles and trials of life. Probably more than any other Bible passage Philippians 4:4-7 has been one my husband, Alan, and I have shared with people who struggle with worry or anxiety: *"Rejoice in the Lord always. I will say it again: Rejoice! Let your gentleness be evident to all. The Lord is near. Do not be anxious about anything, but in everything, by prayer and petition, with thanksgiving, present your requests to God. And the peace of God, which transcends all understanding, will guard your hearts and your minds in Christ Jesus"* (Philippians 4:4-7).

Until recently I would usually quote the verse beginning, *"Do not be anxious about anything...."* But recently, I realized how much better I like including *"The Lord is near. Do not be anxious about anything...."* God is with us — He is our peace. He wants you to quiet yourself, repeat the verse to yourself, recognize God is with you, and speak to your spirit, *"Do not be anxious!"* When you do this, His Word becomes life-giving, your spirit receives encouragement, outside forces seeking to distress you lose their power over you, and an inner victory is achieved by the Spirit of God within you. A powerful testimony of this truth comes to us from Japan, a year after the earthquake and tsunami hit.

God's Nearness in Suffering

Recently I was blessed to watch a news segment on how the spiritual climate in Japan has changed since the 2011 earthquake, with a greater openness to the Gospel now. Yokoyamo Daisuke, a

Japanese evangelist, shared how he was led to move to the affected area and minister to those suffering from the disaster. A number of Christians began to share God's love in practical ways, including helping the owner of a seaweed factory rebuild his plant. Many unsaved began to seek solace in churches and a former gang member, Domae Shogo, who spent twenty-two years in prison, gave his life to Christ. Now he spends his time sharing God's love with many who are still displaced and telling how Christ changed his life. Japan's church leaders united a year after the tsunami, organizing A Celebration of Hope event and bringing Franklin Graham to speak of the hope found in Christ. Twelve thousand attended the three-day event with many coming to know Christ. Local pastors say God is moving in Japan like never before, using a tragic event to open hearts to God's love, grace and salvation. *Out of Suffering Into Glory!* The troubles of life cannot overcome God's love and grace. Even in fearful events, God's glory shines forth through the lives of His people.

Our Light Children's Home in India also just suffered a fearful event in a fire that broke out in the home. Torrential rains had affected area electricity, and the use of burning candles somehow started a fire. None of the children were seriously injured, but many have been traumatized and suffer with fear and anxiety. Our ministry's prayer team has been notified and much prayer is going forth asking God to comfort, restore peace, surround them with His love, and overcome what the enemy sent for harm with God's desire to bring good. One answer already being seen, revealing God's goodness and glory, is the openness of hearts to help the Light Children's Home by sharing love gifts, which will meet some of the needs of the orphanage. The purchase of a generator will eliminate the need for using candles in a home of sixty children. And the daily need for clean water has been met by the installation of a new high capacity water purification system. Out of this hardship, God is touching hearts to share out of the abundance we have in America with His precious children in India. Jesus loves children and is so blessed when we care for the ones dearest to His heart. In all these things He is proving trustworthy as the Father to the fatherless.

As we finish reflecting on trust as the antidote to a troubled heart, I want to share a way I have found to maintain peace and trust in life. This approach is in addition to having a daily quiet time with God and recognizing the importance of God's Word. What I have found helpful is to practice regularly a mental exercise according to the Scripture, "*Cast your cares on the Lord, and he will sustain you* (Psalm 55:22a). There is a slightly different wording in the New Testament, "*Cast all your anxiety on him because he cares for you*" (1 Peter 5:7). I have often thought about this in reference to fishing. I grew up in Massachusetts and enjoyed fishing. How often I remember casting the line out into the water, the further the better. It is too easy to think that the troubles in our lives are ours, which we must carry. But this verse tells us to cast them onto the Lord, in other words, throw them off, release them, let go of the burden of carrying them yourself. I like to visualize what we learn from God's Word, so picture with me taking your worries, anxieties, and fears and releasing them into God's hands — cast them away. He is able to guard what you have entrusted into His loving hands, whether your concern may be your children, health, job, finances, marriage, loved ones, or any other burden. He is able to bear it and desires your heart to be at peace.

Pray with me...

"Lord I trust You with my cares, my worries, my fear and anxieties. I give them to You. I know You don't want me to carry burdens too heavy for me. Thank You that Your will for me is to live each day with the grace given for that day. Thank You for offering me peace and rest as I come to You with all that is on my heart. You are my shepherd and Your word tells me I can rest in green meadows and enjoy quiet streams (Psalm 23:1-2). I believe You will take care of me in all the troubles that come into my life. God, You are good and You are faithful. I trust You. Amen!"

We wait in hope for You, Lord;
You are our help and our shield.
In You our hearts rejoice, for we trust in Your Holy Name.
Psalm 33:20-21

Chapter 7

You Are Never Alone

And I will ask the Father, and he will give you another Counselor
to be with you forever — the Spirit of truth. The world cannot
accept him, because it neither sees him nor knows him.
But you know him, for he lives with you and will be in you.
I will not leave you as orphans;
I will come to you.
John 14:16-18

One of us is cryin' as our hopes and dreams
are led away in chains, and we're left all alone,
One of us is dyin' as our love is slowly lowered in the grave,
Oh and we're left all alone.
But for all of us who journey through the dark abyss of loneliness
There comes a great announcement —
we are never alone.
And Our God is with us, Emmanuel....
As Father and Friend, with us through the end, Emmanuel.

Steven Curtis Chapman — "Our God Is With Us"

The hour of darkness had come. The time of Jesus' greatest trial was upon Him, and He was left alone. As the temple guards came to the Garden of Gethsemane to arrest Jesus, His disciples deserted Him. They fled in fear. They had heard the Master reveal what was to happen when He came to Jerusalem — that He would suffer much, be rejected and killed (Mark 8:31). He had given them the hope that He would rise again in three days. But in facing the armed crowd wielding clubs and swords, His followers lost courage and ran from their master. Jesus was now in the hands of His adversaries, and He was alone.

To face suffering with the sense of being forsaken is one of the greatest hardships you might ever face. Some of you may have been deserted in the past by one who should have remained in your life. Others may have felt abandoned in a time of painful sorrow. Although the darkness of this world and the evil seen in man's inhumanity may at times obscure God's face, the reality is that we are never alone. There is One who came to earth, walked in our shoes, traveled painful paths, and suffered for our sake. Emmanuel — God with us.

To the Israelites God first revealed Himself as Emmanuel, the God who is with us (Isaiah 7:14). He is the God who was present with them in their journeying to the Promised Land, manifested as a cloud by day and a pillar of fire by night. He often revealed His presence in times of greatest need by sending angelic messengers to let His people know they were not alone. He spoke through the prophets of the coming Messiah and the deliverance God would bring to those in bondage to sin and fear. God made a covenant with His chosen people to care for them, to provide for them as a husband would care for His beloved. The prophet Hosea reveals God's covenant keeping promise.

I will betroth you to me forever; I will betroth you in righteousness and justice, in love and compassion. I will betroth you in faithful-ness, and you will acknowledge the Lord.... I will show my love to the one I called "Not my loved one." I will say to those called "Not my people," "You are my people;" and they will say, "You are my God."

Hosea 2:19-20; 23b

Healing from God's Word

God's nature is relational and intimate. In times of greatest need He makes Himself known to those who seek Him. And He offers the healing power of His Word as an anchor to those struggling in life's storms. I witnessed the truth of this in a very personal way in 2006. My husband and I never thought we would face the trial that came upon our family unexpectedly. The phone call came that our daughter's husband had left her. Through tears and anguish the situation unfolded in Jennifer's life that is all too familiar to many in our nation. She was abandoned, deserted by the one who had vowed to remain by her side, *"for better, for worse... to love and to cherish 'till death do us part."* It was a time of great pain for all of us in our family, yet it also became a time of watching God do something amazing in our daughter: He comforted her, brought strength to her, and renewed her faith even in her suffering.

I will never forget one of the most heart stirring occurrences in this trial as Jennifer turned to Jesus with all her heart to find consolation in the grief of her abandonment. God's Word became the lifeline for her soul as she fought for her marriage. Over a week-end, early in her ordeal, she determined to seek God's face as she read and prayed through the entire book of Psalms. The glory of God came into her soul as the Living Word brought nourishment to her inner being. Her face literally shone with the Light of Christ in this time of spiritual transformation. God removed her pain and replaced it with the joy of His presence. I remember her telling me that one of her co-workers asked what had happened to her. He commented that she appeared to be "glowing." God's promise was manifested that *"we, who with unveiled faces all reflect the Lord's glory, are being transformed into his likeness with ever-increasing glory, which comes from the Lord, who is the Spirit"* (2 Corinthians 3:18). Jennifer had received the Holy Spirit's inner healing, peace, joy, and the awareness that she was not alone. God would not forsake her and she could trust Jesus for her deepest needs to be met. *Out of Suffering Into Glory!*

Jennifer has become a powerful woman of God through her suffering. In spite of the eventual divorce, she allowed God's grace to work deeply in her heart. She wrote a letter forgiving her ex-husband, choosing to trust in God for her future, and not allowing any root of bitterness to form. With God's help she moved on with her life. In the years that followed she went on several mission trips to South America where God used her mightily to pray for inner healing for women suffering from emotional pain. I am pleased to share that three years after her divorce God brought a godly man into her life who had been waiting upon God for his spouse. She and Jason have now been married several years and have given my husband and me a precious granddaughter, Lily Grace.

One of the passages of Scripture that ministered to Jennifer in her months of separation was from Isaiah 54:5-8.

> *For your Maker is your husband – the Lord Almighty is his name – the Holy One of Israel is your Redeemer; He is called the God of all the earth. The Lord will call you back as if you were a wife deserted and distressed in spirit – a wife who married young, only to be rejected," says your God." For a brief moment I*

abandoned you, but with deep compassion I will bring you back. In a surge of anger I hid my face from you for a moment but with everlasting kindness I will have compassion on you," says the Lord your Redeemer.

God in His compassionate nature promises to be with those who are abandoned or deserted. His heart is drawn to all those who suffer, and He pours out His love and kindness in amazing ways that bring restoration and healing to broken lives. He is the true source of healing, comfort, and redeeming love to lift up those who have walked through the valley of tears.

Do Not Fear, I Am with You

Have you experienced the pain of being deserted, abandoned, or forsaken? With a divorce rate of over 50% in America, many feel the terrible loss from broken families, and the emotional distress can especially affect children who are the innocent victims in this tragedy. In addition to suffering from divorce, which is more prevalent in western nations, we know that thousands of children around the world have been orphaned, abandoned, or forsaken by parents unable or unwilling to care for them. A number of our children in the Light Children's Home in India have experienced this distress. David expresses hope in the book of Psalms that though some are forsaken by their parents, God will welcome them into His loving arms.

My heart says of you, "Seek his face!" Your face, Lord, I will seek. Do not hide your face from me, do not turn your servant away in anger; you have been my helper. Do not reject me or forsake me, O God my Savior. Though my father and mother forsake me, the Lord will receive me.

Psalm 27:8-10

Jesus Himself declared how important children are to His kingdom.

People were bringing little children to Jesus to have him touch them, but the disciples rebuked them. When Jesus saw this, he was indignant. He said to them, "Let the little children come to me, and do not hinder them, for the kingdom of God belongs to such as these. I tell you the truth, anyone who will not receive the kingdom of God like a little child will never enter it." And he took the children in his arms, put his hands on them and blessed them.

Mark 10:13-16

All around the world God is calling His followers to establish orphanages and ministries to care for abandoned children. I know several people in ministry who are working in Brazil, Calcutta, Kenya, and Haiti to care for "the least of these" (Matthew 25:40). Their hearts feel the pain of these forsaken ones and they have obeyed the admonition from James 1:27 — *"Religion that God our Father accepts as pure and faultless is this: to look after orphans and widows in their distress and to keep oneself from being polluted by the world."*

I became an orphan at age twenty-five when my father died. Even though I was grown and married, I still felt a sense of abandonment deep within. At the time I did not understand God's purpose in allowing my pain—yet, I found comfort and strength in the promises of God's Word. Little did I know that out of my own suffering God would be glorified in bringing about His plans to care for others who suffer. This is the glory of God's redemptive purposes in suffering. Again I repeat that God does not waste our sorrows. He will not waste your sorrows. He is with you through them and wants you to seek Him in your pain. Be encouraged with these words.

So do not fear, for I am with you; do not be dismayed, for I am your God. I will strengthen you and help you; I will uphold you with my righteous right hand.

Isaiah 41:10

The LORD is a refuge for the oppressed, a stronghold in times of trouble. Those who know your name will trust in you, for you, LORD, have never forsaken those who seek you.

Psalm 9:9-10

The Way Out of Loneliness

Over the past ten years I have had numerous dreams of rescuing children. Several dreams had tornadoes coming and I took up small children and held them to my chest and found a place of refuge in a basement and a stronghold to wrap my arms around. Another dream had an evil man trying to take a child out of a car, but I held onto the child to keep him safe. A vivid dream several years ago came as a sign from God leading to our present involvement in India. A child was thrown away, abandoned in a trash dumpster, and in my dream I climbed in and rescued the child. The next morning when I woke there was an email from the Light Children's Home, asking us to please help them. It was not a coincidence. The director's name is John and our son's name is John. And the name of the orphanage is the Light Children's Home, and I love to speak and teach on Christ as the Light of the world. God enables us to be His hands, His voice, and His heart to those who are suffering. He has given my husband and me the privilege of being the spiritual mother and father for children who had once been abandoned or forsaken but now are cared for at the Light Children's Home. Their loneliness is now eased by living in community with Christian "parents" at the orphanage.

Please believe there is a purpose and redemptive plan even for loneliness. My sister is an amazing woman who has carried much pain as I have from our childhood. She also is often afflicted with deep loneliness. But today she is one who continually seeks to minister and care for those on life's margins — the sick, the imprisoned, those suffering emotional distress. I am so proud of how she pushes through her pain and seeks ways to turn it for good in touching others with God's love. So though you may suffer for a season, God is with you. He is your Redeemer and He will use your suffering for His Kingdom purposes as you surrender it to Him.

Jesus understands this pain of loneliness. The redemption of God's purposes for suffering is seen in what Jesus endured on the cross in being forsaken by His Father. Already betrayed by one of His disciples, deserted by His followers, denied by one of His closest friends. Now the loneliness of having even His Father turn from Him crushes Him.

> *At the sixth hour darkness came over the whole land until the ninth hour. And at the ninth hour Jesus cried out in a loud voice, "Eloi, Eloi, lama sabachthani?" — which means, "My God, my God, why have you forsaken me?"*
>
> Mark 15:33-34

The Son of God forsaken by His Father? The One who is perfect in holiness, all-good, righteous, and just could not look on the Lamb upon whom the sins of the world were placed. Jesus' pain and sorrow bought us freedom and forgiveness. His heart possessed love that would radically transform the world. Never had the world witnessed the sacrificial love of Agape — the love from the heart of God. *"This is love: not that we loved God, but that he loved us and sent his Son as an atoning sacrifice for our sins"* (1 John 4:10). The restoration of the Son with the Father came after Jesus' resurrection from the dead. It was the ultimate portrayal of "out of suffering into glory." He knows your pain. He knows those times when loneliness comes upon you. He endured it also. But there is promised restoration and release from suffering for those who look to the Savior. And the hope of the glory of God comes to those who patiently endure suffering.

Why Has All This Happened to Us?

In our fallen world the anguish of being forsaken often comes through selfishness, inflicting sorrow on innocent victims. Yet hardships and trials may also be the result of those who choose to go their own way, refusing to follow the way God has laid out for them in the Ten Commandments and in the teachings of Jesus.

The Hebrew nation experienced a time when they felt forsaken by God, when their enemies oppressed them. They had forsaken the One and only True God and fallen into spiritual idolatry. In their distress, they turned to God and cried out for relief. And in love and faithfulness, God heard their cries and answered.

When the angel of the Lord appeared to Gideon, he said, "The Lord is with you, mighty warrior." "But sir," Gideon replied, "if the Lord is with us, why has all this happened to us? Where

are all his wonders that our fathers told us about when they said,
'Did not the Lord bring us up out of Egypt?' But now the Lord
*has **abandoned** us and put us into the hand of Midian." The*
Lord turned to him and said, "Go in the strength you have and
save Israel out of Midian's hand. Am I not sending you?" "But
Lord," Gideon asked, "how can I save Israel? My clan is the
weakest in Manasseh, and I am the least in my family. " The
Lord answered, "I will be with you, and you will strike down all
the Midianites together."

Judges 6:12-16

God heard their cries and raised up Gideon as leader over the Israelites. The nation turned their hearts back to God and repented of idolatry, and God brought about deliverance from their enemies. Over and over again throughout their history God's chosen people turned from God, fell into unfaithfulness, and brought on themselves the consequences of their idolatry. Many today need to search within to see if there are any idols they've allowed in their lives. Without realizing it, some have brought pain into their lives through unintentional idolatry. As a warning to the early church, we have the words of John, the beloved disciple, *"We know that the Son of God has come and has given us understanding, so that we may know him who is true. And we are in him who is true – even in his Son Jesus Christ. He is the true God and eternal life. Dear children, keep yourselves from idols"* (1 John 5:20-21).

God our Father watches over His children—even those who stray from walking in His ways. Rebellion and disobedience to His commands can make us feel abandoned by God even though we are the ones who have abandoned God. In His love and justice there are times He allows natural consequences to bring us to the place of having no one else to look to but God. Psalm 22:24 tells us, *"For he* has not despised or disdained the suffering of the afflicted one; he has not hidden his face from him but has listened to his cry for help." I remember in my teen years the sense of being alone, feeling forsaken by God and others as I suffered great emotional distress. I really wasn't abandoned, but I felt that way. At times I despaired of life and even felt suicidal in my anguish. But it was <u>my</u> rebellion and refusal to surrender my life to God that had resulted in my plight. In 1974, His love rescued me as I gave up control of my life and cried out to Jesus. I was not alone. I had not been abandoned. My spiritually blind eyes couldn't see the open arms of Jesus until I repented and turned from my selfish ways. Paul's words in Ephesians 2:1-10 beautifully describe the grace of God which redeems sinners. Praise God!

As for you, you were dead in your transgressions and sins, in which you used to live when you followed the ways of this world and of the ruler of the kingdom of the air, the spirit who is now at work in those who are disobedient. All of us also lived among them at one time, gratifying the cravings of our sinful nature and following its desires and thoughts. Like the rest, we were by nature objects of wrath. But because of his great love for us, God, who is rich in mercy, made us alive with Christ even when we were dead in transgressions – it is by grace you have been saved. And God raised us up with Christ and seated us with him in the heavenly realms in Christ Jesus, in order that in the coming ages he might show the incomparable riches of his grace, expressed in his kindness to us in Christ Jesus. For it is by grace you have been saved, through faith – and this not from yourselves, it is the gift of God – not by works, so that no one can boast. For we are God's workmanship, created in Christ Jesus to do good works, which God prepared in advance for us to do.

Ephesians 2:1-10

This section of God's Word is one of the most powerful Biblical explanations of God's plan of salvation by grace through faith. In humility you may have to admit as I did that, yes, I was dead in my transgressions and sins. Yes, I was disobedient. Yes, I lived seeking to gratify my sinful nature and I was an object of wrath. But there is no sin so great that God's grace cannot forgive. No place where we can hide that God's great love won't come and rescue us. No rebellion too great that God will not receive us to Himself as we turn back and repent of our sins. Satan, the cruel enemy of mankind, wanted to destroy my life and keep me forever separated from the love of God. But God's redemptive heart brought me back into His arms of saving grace. His arms are open to you, dear reader.

Do you still carry the pain of being forsaken by a loved one? Do you mistakenly feel that God has forsaken you? Know this truth — God loves you and He <u>is</u> with you. You are not alone, though the enemy may try to hide God's presence from you. The writer of the New Testament book of Hebrews declares to you, *"God has said, 'Never will I leave you; never will I forsake you.' So we say with confidence, 'The Lord is my helper; I will not be afraid. What can man do to me?'"* (Hebrews 13:5b-6)

Pray with me...

Father, I need You. I am desperate to know I am not alone. In this world You are my advocate. Though all forsake me, You will not forsake me. You stay by my side, and walk with me in my trials and suffering. In all that has happened to me, You are able to use it for good. You can redeem all the pain in my life for Your purposes. Help me yield my life more fully to You. Help me forgive those who have caused me pain. I choose to extend grace to them as You did while You hung on the cross. Lord, bring me to Your side and help me believe Your Word that there is nothing that can separate me from Your love (Romans 8:39). I am not alone in this world. You are my God and I am yours forever. Amen!

So do not fear,
for I am with you;
do not be dismayed,
for I am your God.
Isaiah 41:10

Offering grace before mealtime at the Light Children's Home

*Alan, Sally and Tara Crumb with the Light Home children
lined up for their walk to school*

Sally sharing a message of hope to women of southeast India

*Prayer offered before sharing God's Word at meeting for Leprosy victims
(Alan, Sally and Tara Crumb)*

Alan and Sally praying for the leprosy victims

Leprosy victims praising the Lord after the proclamation of God's Word of hope

*Alan and Sally with the Director of Light Children's Home
John Samuel Kim and his wife Sravanthi*

*Light Children posing for group picture — Front row: James Park,
John Samuel, Sravanthi, Sally & Alan Keiran and Carly Bailey*

Chapter 8

Pain: All Things Work For Good

I believe pain and suffering can either be
a prison or a prism.
The tests of life are not to break us but to make us.
Tim Hansel, *You Gotta Keep Dancin'*

Brokenness. The human body endures much in the course of a lifetime. Falling off a glacier into a crevasse is not one of the most common trials. 1974—the Palisade Glacier of the Sierra Nevada. Summit Expedition founder Tim Hansel and friends were experiencing the beauty and wonder of God's creation when they encountered the unexpected. Tim lost his footing and fell off the mountain. Miraculously he finished the climb, hiked out with his friends, and returned home where his body went into shock.

So began his journey of a life filled with chronic pain. Doctors diagnosed fractures, crushed discs, and massive soft tissue damage of the ligaments, tendons, and muscles in his back. Tim's injuries were beyond the possibility of repair and led to traumatic, deteriorating arthritis. Out of this suffering Tim wrote about what he learned from the pain and in 1985 published *You Gotta Keep Dancin'*, a book that has powerfully impacted my life.

We all understand pain to some degree. It is common to human existence whether its source is physical, emotional, mental, or spiritual. What have you learned from pain? Is it a friend or foe? Much wisdom has come into my life from Tim Hansel's book. Mercifully, I have not endured a lot of physical pain in my life, but Hansel's words have brought great hope and encouragement in the midst of my lifelong emotional pain. From Tim's journal in his book....

Spring 1985 ~ Pain again. Or should I say still. I haven't slept through a whole night for almost nine weeks. After ten years, I'm weary of it. Every inch of me wants a break. I feel like a butterfly that is still alive, but pinned wiggling to a board. Aspirin, pain pills, prayer. More prayer, more aspirin, more pain pills. Sometimes nothing seems to work.... Yet, you are enough God. "This priceless treasure we hold, so to speak, in common earthenware- to show that the splendid power of it belongs to God and not to us.... We are puzzled but never in despair....We may be knocked down but we are never knocked out! Every day we experience something of the death of Jesus. So that we may also show the power of the life of Jesus in these bodies of ours" (2 Corinthians 4:7-10, Phillips). You are enough God![1]

The Agony of Crucifixion

Jesus understands pain and brokenness. He knows everything you've gone through in your life and is in Heaven interceding for you as you encounter pain and suffering. The road back to the glory

of Heaven first took Jesus to the cross where He suffered the excruciating pain of crucifixion. Leading up to this, Jesus was beaten,
scourged, and struck by the very people He came to save. The
prophet Isaiah gives this description of the suffering servant. *"His
appearance was so disfigured beyond that of any man and his form marred
beyond human likeness"* (Isaiah 52:14). The cruelty of the Roman sol-
diers released on the Savior one of the harshest methods of punishment designed for slow torture. A whip studded with bones or iron
pellets would have been used for the scourging, which resulted in
the flesh ripping from the back of the victim. There would have
been tremendous loss of blood from the forty lashes. Many who
faced crucifixion didn't survive the scourging. Jesus did and was
then led to Golgotha, the place where He was crucified. Here He
suffered the extreme pain of the nails driven through his hands and
feet. These same hands that once touched and healed multitudes
now endured excruciating torture for love's sake.

Stephen M. Miller explains the horror of Roman crucifixion
in this way. "The suffering of crucifixion came in many forms.
Probably of least concern to any victim was the public disgrace.
More immediate concerns were the pain of the nails, along with the
persistence of gnats, flies, and birds the victim could not ward off.
As the hours, and often days, dragged on, the victim suffered thirst,
hunger, exhaustion, congestion, and difficulty in breathing. It often
took about three days to die—sometimes longer."[2] The victims of
crucifixion would actually die from a combination of shock, loss of
blood, exhaustion, asphyxiation, and finally heart failure.

Because of what He suffered on the cross, Jesus became the
source of healing for all who call on His name. This fulfilled the
word of the prophet Isaiah who wrote of the servant who would

bear the iniquities of the people and bring healing to those who are suffering. *"Surely he took up our infirmities and carried our sorrows, yet we considered him stricken by God, smitten by him, and afflicted. But he was pierced for our transgressions, he was crushed for our iniquities, the punishment that brought us peace was upon him, and by his wounds we are healed"* (Isaiah 53:4-5).

The Apostle Peter quotes this passage from Isaiah about the hope for healing as he instructs the church to live in righteousness. *"He himself bore our sins in his body on the tree, so that we might die to sins and live for righteousness; by his wounds you have been healed"* (1 Peter 2:24). Imagine living at the time of Jesus and being witness to the incredible healing miracles He accomplished during His three years of ministry. Jesus began his ministry *"preaching the good news of the kingdom, and healing every disease and sickness among the people. News about him spread all over Syria, and people brought to him all who were ill with various diseases, those suffering severe pain, the demon-possessed, those having seizures, and the paralyzed, and he healed them"* (Matthew 4:23-24).

Have you ever studied the healing miracles in the Bible? My husband and I began to study them after my husband received an unexpected supernatural healing from a sprained ankle. We were just beginning in ministry in 1979 pastoring a small church in up-state New York. My husband during a soccer game had sprained his ankle; it was swollen, painful, and black and blue. A friend of ours came to visit over the weekend and shared with us that she believed our God still heals today. She asked to pray for Alan's ankle and as she prayed, Alan saw a flash of bright light and immediately all the symptoms disappeared. He was totally healed. Our eyes were opened to a whole new understanding of the reality of the Bible as relevant for today. Our spiritual hunger for the super-natural grew as we recognized that *"Jesus Christ is the same yester-day and today and forever"* (Hebrews 13:8). He healed two thousand years ago and He still heals today. Over the past thirty years Alan and I have received from God a number of healings in our bodies. We have also prayed in faith for many who were sick and have seen God do amazing things.

The Prayer Chair

One of the most powerful healings from God took place in our living room in 2007 in what we call the "prayer chair." Our dear friend Chico, a regular member of our home group Bible study, had come to our meeting with great concern, sharing that he was diagnosed with four blockages in his heart, needed surgery, and had a job that did not provide health coverage. In faith our group gathered around Chico, laid hands on him, and began to pray. As God's Holy Spirit led us in this time of prayer, we declared the truth of God's Word over our friend.

"God, You forgive all our sins and heal all our diseases, and Your Word tells us that in Your name believers will place hands on sick people, and they will get well. For by Your wounds we have been healed. We agree with your promise that the prayer offered in faith will make the sick person well. Thank You that the prayer of a righteous man is powerful and effective! Teach us how to walk in the healing and power you have provided. Amen!" (Psalm 103:3, Mark 16:17-18, 1 Peter 2:24, James 5:14-16)

The compassion of Jesus flowed in our home that night as we cried out to God for our friend — for his heart to be healed — and as we prayed, God moved in response. Chico later shared with us that he felt a hand touching his heart as if massaging it. He received God's love and healing of past emotional pain. (Previously we had met with Chico and led him in prayers of forgiveness for those who had wounded him during his childhood years. Prayer ministers will readily admit that unforgiveness hinders God's flow of healing. There are numerous testimonies of those who have received healing after forgiving those who have hurt them.) In our ministry with Chico, he knew God had been present and had touched him in a powerful way. Over the next few weeks, he went back for appointments with several doctors and each was surprised that upon examination they could now find no blockages. One doctor even dared to state that a miracle had happened to Chico. Yeah God!

The Mystery of God in Suffering

Isn't it wonderful to see God's Word come true? Our God is awesome. He is worthy of praise and His goodness is everlasting. Yet, as incredible as it is when you experience a supernatural healing — and I hope that you have witnessed this in your life — the reality is that not everyone is healed. There is a mystery to the ways of God. In times of sickness we may long to receive a miraculous touch from God but feel hurt and disappointed when God seems to pass us by. Rev. Frances MacNutt, founder of Christian Healing Ministries, is a man who has been mightily used by God in healing ministry for decades. In his ministry he has seen a number of people suffering from illnesses or disease who receive instantaneous healing. Others receive healing as a result of long-term prayer over weeks or months. Then there are those, who for unknown reasons, are not healed. Yet, to those who live in devotion and commitment to the lordship of Christ, these individuals will declare that their desire is to see God glorified in their suffering. And they hope their lives will testify of God's sovereign purposes in the midst of their affliction.

I often read testimonies of those who have passed through pain and sorrow and come through stronger in their faith. We all need to be encouraged to know that suffering is not in vain. I have a file folder in my home filled with stories and articles which bear witness to the truth of God's promise in Romans 8:28, *"In all things God works for the good of those who love him, who have been called according to His purpose."* Numerous authors also have written to testify that in their sufferings God achieves His redemptive purposes. Their lives reveal that they have drawn closer to God in their trials and He has been faithful to walk with them even in the deepest valleys.

Bob Sorge, a worship leader and pastor, came under a severe trial in 1992 when his throat was damaged by laser treatment during surgery to remove a throat ulcer. Extreme pain continued after surgery and he could only whisper for short periods. His vocation as worship leader and pastor depended on his ability to speak, so Bob and his wife entered into a time of asking God "why," of struggling to understand pain and affliction and crying out, "Where are you God in my suffering?"

When we pass through pain and suffering, we can't help but ask "Why God?" We do a self-evaluation and look within, wondering if the trial is a punishment or the result of a lack of faith. Bob Sorge prayed, "Lord, I've prayed, I've praised, I've repented, I've fasted, I've rebuked, I've surrendered. I've read books, quoted Scripture, spent time in Your presence, I've reconciled with everyone who may have had a problem with me."[3] And what do you do when

God is silent? One thing you must not do is turn away from God. Run to Him. Run to the cross. See Jesus hanging there taking your pain, in agony for love's sake. Look into His eyes burning with love and know you are not alone in your pain and affliction. Christ hung on the cross, suffering severe pain, and it was <u>not</u> wasted. God accomplished the greatest purpose in the crucifixion—the forgiveness of our sins, the reconciliation of a fallen race, the restoration of mankind into fellowship with God our Heavenly Father. These lyrics give beautiful expression to God's amazing redemptive purposes for Christ's death.

> *"Father, forgive them," my Savior prayed —*
> *Even while His lifeblood flowed fast away*
> *Praying for sinners while in such woe —*
> *No one but Jesus ever loved so*
> *Blessed Redeemer, precious Redeemer*
> *Seems now I see Him on Calvary's tree*
> *Wounded and bleeding, for sinners pleading —*
> *Blind and unheeding, dying for me*
> Casting Crowns—"Blessed Redeemer"

I have received much encouragement from Bob Sorge. His suffering has resulted in a life of deep intimacy with God out of which he has authored many books over the past twenty years, including *The Fire of Delayed Answers* and its sequel *The Fire of God's Love*. He has also written a commentary on the book of Job, entitled *Pain, Perplexity, and Promotion: a Prophetic Interpretation of the Book of Job.* Job is known to readers of Scripture as a righteous man who underwent great loss and suffering but found restoration through humble acceptance of God's purpose in suffering. Suffering proves character, refining those who still love and serve God when tested by the fire of affliction. In your suffering, are you able to declare, "God, I still love you even though I am not healed. I will trust in your sovereign purposes in allowing this trial in my life"?

Lives of Selfless Service

Because of our ministry to orphans in India, I have long admired Amy Carmichael who was a missionary to India in the early 20th century. This young Irish woman was used by God to rescue dozens of orphans from prostitution at Hindu temples. Yet in 1931 she was injured in a serious fall and became an invalid suffering with severe arthritis. During this time she continued to direct the ministry of Dohnavur, ministering the love of Christ to children. In her last twenty years of life, she continued as spiritual mother to hundreds of children and wrote numerous devotional books greatly inspiring Christians to lives of selfless devotion and service to God.

Another testimony of redemptive suffering is seen in the life of Australian motivational speaker Nick Vujicic, who was born without arms or legs. His is a life of incredible perseverance with overcoming great hardship. As a child he faced enormous challenges, due to his disability, along with the great emotional pain of being different. At one point in his pre-teen years severe depression caused him to consider suicide. But the love of his parents and the hope he found in Christ gave him strength to rise above his handicaps. At the age of nineteen, Nick began to travel and speak, sharing how his relationship with Jesus Christ enabled him to see meaning in his pain. "I found the purpose of my existence, and also the purpose of my circumstance. There's a purpose for why you're in the fire," he writes on his website for his non-profit organization

LifeWithoutLimbs.org.[4] Nick testifies that God is with us in our struggles. He also states that faith and trust in Jesus Christ will enable us to see the pain in our life used for good and the accomplishing of God's purposes. Since 2001 he has traveled to twenty-five countries as an inspirational speaker encouraging those who suffer to find hope and meaning in a personal relationship with Christ. In February 2012 Nick was blessed to enter into marriage to his beautiful soul-mate Kanae Miyahara.

A friend of mine, Cheryl Owens Patterson, has lived with cancer for fifteen years. She has become a woman of great spiritual wisdom in this time as she presses into her Lord and Savior for grace for each day. She wrote to me recently, "I'm thrilled that God has allowed me to walk for fifteen years with cancer, because He constantly reveals more of His character to me, which is awesome!" She also shared her unique way of praying that I believe will be an encouragement to many. The principle upon which she prays comes from the instruction Graham Cooke gives to those living with a disease or illness. "I am not fighting a disease (or sickness). Rather, I am submitting myself into all the goodness and power of God." My friend says she loves this because it changes the energy in her spirit. Instead of having to extend energy out for healing, all she has to do is submit into God's goodness and power.

As I thought about this truth I saw that we have before us the imagery of two rivers for those facing illness. One is the River of Life flowing full of God's goodness, life and healing. The other is a raging river flowing with torrents threatening to overwhelm us. I saw myself choosing to rest in God's River of Life focusing on His power and goodness whereby I can trust Him with my life. In the other river our circumstances may cause us great stress and anxiety because we uncertain how to fight the diagnosis we've been given.

God says, "Trust Me. Seek Me… rest in My love and care for you."

Pain, chronic or acute. We will all suffer from pain in our life-time. For those who are suffering with long-term pain, my heart goes out to you. I understand that it is not easy to live day to day with ongoing pain. And simple clichés are not always enough to lift your spirit. But there is One who is by your side, who has also ex-perienced pain, who loves you with pure, perfect love and will not leave you. Heaven awaits those who have put their trust in Jesus and it is a place with no pain. Do not let go of your hope. I end this chapter on pain with some of the precious promises I have held onto in my own suffering. May God bless you as you allow His Word to bring you life and strength.

Steps To Take To Apply Truths From God's Word

Hold onto God's Word of truth—let it be the foundation of your life

Be cheerful no matter what; pray all the time; thank God no matter what happens. This is the way God wants you who belong to Christ Jesus to live (1 Thessalonians 5:16-18, MSG).

Be encouraged by Christ's suffering

Fix [your] eyes on Jesus, the author and perfecter of [your] faith, who for the joy set before him endured the cross (Hebrews 12:2).

Meditate on God's love for you

Because of the Lord's great love we are not consumed, for his compassions never fail. They are new every morning; great is your faithfulness (Lamentations 3:22-23).

Remember your life bears witness to those who don't believe

Let your light shine before men, that they may see your good deeds and praise your Father in heaven (Matthew 5:16).

Put your hope in the Lord

Find rest, O my soul, in God alone; my hope comes from him (Psalm 62:5).

Find ways to laugh daily

A happy heart makes the face cheerful, but heartache crushes the spirit... A cheerful look brings joy to the heart, and good news gives health to the bones (Proverbs 15:13, 30).

Find beauty and joy in the gift of each new day

Let the heavens rejoice, let the earth be glad; let the sea resound, and all that is in it; let the fields be jubilant, and everything in them. Then all the trees of the forest will sing for joy; they will sing before the Lord (Psalm 96:11-12).

Look for ways to give and serve others

If you spend yourselves in behalf of the hungry and satisfy the needs of the oppressed, then your light will rise in the darkness, and your night will become like the noonday. The Lord will guide you always; he will satisfy your needs in a sun-scorched land and will strengthen your frame (Isaiah 58:10-11).

Avoid too much self-focus

For Christ's love compels us, because we are convinced that one died for all, and therefore all died. And he died for all, that those who live should no longer live for themselves but for him who died for them and was raised again (2 Corinthians 5:14-15).

Cultivate deep fellowship with the Lord

I want to know Christ and the power of his resurrection and the fellowship of sharing in his sufferings (Philippians 3:10).

Chapter 9

Life Conquers Death

For as in Adam all die, so in Christ all will be made alive.
But each in his own turn: Christ, the firstfruits; then,
when he comes, those who belong to him. Then the end will come,
when he hands over the kingdom to God the Father after he has
destroyed all dominion, authority and power. For he must reign
until he has put all his enemies under his feet.
The last enemy to be destroyed is death.
1 Corinthians 15:22-26

Death is an enemy, but it is no longer the victor. Christ died. But He was raised from the dead. He defeated our greatest enemy and He lives forever. As followers of Jesus Christ we also gain, through our unity with Him, everything that He accomplished while fulfilling His God-ordained mission. This is cause for rejoicing! Do not let your eyes stay so focused on your earthbound existence that you forget that each day we can rejoice that sin and death have been vanquished and our Savior lives!

You have journeyed through the life of Christ as we have followed Him on the path of suffering leading up to the cross. Go back with me to Good Friday, the day we celebrate the greatest rescue operation ever accomplished in our world. Remember the words from Hebrews 5:8, "*Although he was a son, he learned obedience from what he suffered and, once made perfect, he became the source of eternal salvation for all who obey him.*" In all His temptations and suffering, Jesus did not sin. He was obedient to His Heavenly Father and did what was right and good and just. He did not listen to the ruler of this world (Satan). He kept His eyes fixed on His Father. He followed His voice and persevered through His trials. Suffering proves those who suffer, and it refines them. Suffering helps to cleanse people from the common reactions seen in this world of anger, self-pity, and bitterness. We have a choice in our afflictions — we can be made bitter or better. Let us choose to be better by God's grace.

Men and woman held in bondage to sin have been under the power of Satan since creation. In the passage below, God's plan of redemption is soon to be realized in God's Son laying down His life for those lost in their sins. Our Savior is about to complete His mission as revealed by the Prophet Isaiah.

> *He was arrested and sentenced and led off to die, and no one cared about his fate. He was put to death for the sins of our people. He was placed in a grave with those who are evil, he was buried with the rich, even though he had never committed a crime or ever told a lie. The Lord says, it was my will that he should suffer; his death was a sacrifice to bring forgiveness.... After a life of suffering, he will again have joy; he will know that he did not suffer in vain. My devoted servant, with whom I am pleased, will bear the punishment of many and for his sake I will forgive them. And so I will give him a place of honor, a place among the great and powerful. He willingly gave his life and shared the fate of*

evil men. He took the place of many sinners and prayed that they might be forgiven.

Isaiah 53:8-12 (GNT)

Sin is a powerful enemy. I still remember the sinfulness of my heart in my years of rebellion and the great inner conflict between my selfish desires, my deceived mind, and my guilty conscience. Although I was caught in this state mainly during my teenage years, I still view them as wasted years. But my God is a redeemer. We were once all dead in our sins (Ephesians 2:1-2), unaware that we were in slavery to the ruler of this world. Without a Savior we had no hope for escaping our sinful state. No hope of eternal life. Paul, the apostle, also remembers the condition of his soul as he writes to Titus, *"At one time we too were foolish, disobedient, deceived and enslaved by all kinds of passions and pleasures. We lived in malice and envy, being hated and hating one another. But when the kindness and love of God our Savior appeared, he saved us, not because of righteous things we had done, but because of his mercy"* (Titus 3:3-5a).

Jesus Came to Die

God placed on the cross the One who would overthrow the ruler of this world and restore mankind back to the intimate re-lationship that once existed with Him in the Garden of Eden. Our Father in Heaven is a holy and just God who created man for fel-lowship. That fellowship was broken by disobedience and needed to be restored. A sin barrier separated man from God. As God's rescue plan unfolds, Jesus — the Lamb of God — is to be offered as the perfect sacrifice. With this offering of the sinless Son of Man, you and I have the punishment for our sins paid for. You can be purchased back, along with the entire human race, through faith in Christ. The atonement allows us to be "at one" with God. Restored. Hallelujah!

Reflect with me now on the greatest injustice ever seen in the history of the world. Cruel, sinful men placed on the cross the Savior of the world. The holy and righteous Son of Man suffered the agony of crucifixion for the sake of love. He endured the wrath of God, the physical pain in His body, the weight of the world's sins, and the inner sorrow of being forsaken by His Father. He had been on the cross since the third hour of the day (9 am). Mankind was about to witness redemption.

> *It was now about the sixth hour, and darkness came over the whole land until the ninth hour, for the sun stopped shining. And the curtain of the temple was torn in two. Jesus called out with a loud voice, "Father, into your hands I commit my spirit." When he had said this, he breathed his last. The centurion, seeing what had happened, praised God and said, "Surely this was a righteous man."*

> Luke 23:44-47

Since the time of Moses, atonement for sins was made by the offering of the lamb as a blood sacrifice. Forgiveness of sins was only possible through the shedding of blood. Just before the sacrifice, the priest would blow the shofar, and the lamb would be sacrificed at the ninth hour. All who heard it knew the lamb had died for their sins. At the exact moment of the afternoon sacrifice, "Jesus said, 'It is finished.' With that, he bowed his head and gave up his spirit" (John 19:30). The perfect Lamb of God had given His life for the sins of the world.

The Curtain Is Torn

Matthew tells us that at that very moment the temple curtain *"was torn in two from top to bottom. The earth shook and the rocks split.... When the centurion and those with him who were guarding Jesus saw the earthquake and all that had happened, they were terrified, and exclaimed, 'Surely he was the Son of God!'"* (Matthew 27:51,54) The Son of God fulfilled His mission. He came to offer His life for sinful man to reconcile us to God. The tearing of the temple curtain powerfully revealed that no longer was there anything separating man from God. No longer would sin keep us from our Holy God. As Paul writes to the Corinthian church, *"We implore you on Christ's behalf: Be reconciled to God. God made him who had no sin to be sin for us, so that in him we might become the righteousness of God"* (2 Corinthians 5:20-21). The way is now open into the Holy of Holies where we are able to come into God's presence by accepting the righteousness of Christ. In the book of Colossians Paul tells us this truth, *"now he has reconciled you by Christ's physical body through death to present you holy in his sight, without blemish and free from accusation"* (Colossians 1:22). Hallelujah!

Rejoice! Christ's death has opened the way to Heaven. He has removed the sin barrier, and we can run into the loving arms of our Holy Father. Hear Him say to you...

My children, come... come into My presence. I love you and I long for you. The way is open and there is nothing to fear. Do not let the enemy keep you from knowing Me fully. I have created you for fellowship with Me and to know Me like no other. I want you to have no fear, but know that in My presence is perfect peace and perfect joy. Do not listen to the father of lies who would keep you from this blessed privilege I offer you. Come to Me. Come and know true freedom and joy. There is everything you need in My presence. I long to have you enjoy walking with Me in the secret place where I dwell. Trust Me and do not fear. Yes, I am a God of Holy Fearsomeness, but I am also a God who loves My children and wants to care for them as a Shepherd for His sheep and a Father for His children. Come and walk with Me. Hear My voice calling you to come away and spend time in the secret place of My presence. Come, My beloved, and know Me.

Victory Over Death

God wants you to know His voice (John 10:3-4:16). He wants you to distinguish His voice from others. Daily He speaks through His Word and through the quietness of communion with Him. He wants you to enjoy a loving relationship with Him. Jesus taught His followers, *"I tell you the truth, whoever hears my word and believes him who sent me has eternal life and will not be condemned; he has crossed over from death to life"* (John 5: 24). Your life has been redeemed from sin and death. Because Jesus died in your place, you no longer need to fear judgment; you no longer need to fear death. You have crossed over from death to life, from the Kingdom of darkness to the Kingdom of light. I love these words from Paul telling us of our new standing, *"For he has rescued us from the dominion of darkness and brought us into the kingdom of the Son he loves, in whom we have redemption, the forgiveness of sins"* (Colossians 1:13-14).

For three days Jesus remained in darkness, hidden from the world. We do not know fully what occurred in the days between His death and resurrection. Several scriptures refer to this time and give us some understanding that the forces of darkness were profoundly defeated. *"Having canceled the written code, with its regulations, that was against us and that stood opposed to us; he took it away, nailing it to the cross. And having disarmed the powers and authorities, he made a public spectacle of them, triumphing over them by the cross"* (Colossians 2:14-15). For certain, we know He was victorious over the powers of darkness as evidenced by His resurrection from the dead.

> *On the first day of the week, very early in the morning, the women took the spices they had prepared and went to the tomb. They found the stone rolled away from the tomb, but when they entered, they did not find the body of the Lord Jesus. While they were wondering about this, suddenly two men in clothes that gleamed like lightning stood beside them. In their fright the women bowed down with their faces to the ground, but the men said to them, "Why do you look for the living among the dead? He is not here; **he has risen!** Remember how he told you, while he was still with you in Galilee: 'The Son of Man must be delivered into the hands of sinful men, be crucified and on the third day be raised again.'" Then they remembered his words.*
>
> Luke 24:1-8

Rejoice... He Is Risen

He Has Risen! The greatest news ever announced cheered the hearts of His grieving followers. Jesus was no longer in the tomb. Death could hold Him no longer. God's power of resurrection life brought our Savior back from the dead. With great joy His followers witnessed His appearing as they gathered together — uncertain about their future. *"On the evening of that first day of the week, when the disciples were together, with the doors locked for fear of the Jews, Jesus came and stood among them and said, 'Peace be with you!' After he said this, he showed them his hands and side. The disciples were overjoyed when they saw the Lord. Again Jesus said, 'Peace be with you! As the Father has sent me, I am sending you.' And with that he breathed on them and said, 'Receive the Holy Spirit. If you forgive anyone his sins, they are forgiven; if you do not forgive them, they are not forgiven'"* (John 20:19-23).

Can you imagine the joy in that room? Their beloved Lord had been killed. They had watched Him brutally murdered and grieved His death. Now He stood before them. *"Peace be with you,"* He said. The peace He declared was the "shalom" of heaven, the peace of being reconciled to God, the peace of a soul at rest — no longer under condemnation for transgressions. This peace will change your life if you truly comprehend where you stand with God because of Jesus Christ's death and resurrection. Receive this peace. Receive His Holy Spirit. Let His breath come upon you by the Spirit to infuse in you new life… the life of the Spirit… life which overcomes death.

Pause to allow God to minister His LIFE to you by His Spirit to refresh and renew you. "Father, I am yours. I want your resurrection power in my life. Breathe on me Holy Spirit. Bring me Your peace and joy. I repent of my sins, forgive me by the blood of Christ. Remove from me sin and the penalty of death, and give me everlasting life through my faith in Jesus Christ. I thank You for Your amazing grace."

The Resurrection Is No Myth

Because Jesus rose from the dead, His disciples overcame fear and found courage to joyfully accept the mission of spreading the Good News of salvation through Christ. Many theologians have proven the resurrection of Christ with the recognition that each of the apostles courageously undertook the work of bringing the message of reconciliation to the Father through Christ's death on the cross without fear of imprisonment or death. No one would die for a lie, and each of the apostles, except Judas and John, were martyred during the years of the early church.

The incredible growth of Christianity over the past two thousand years is because we have a risen Savior. Jesus is our living Lord. He continues to rule and reign in the Kingdom of God and has given us the responsibility and mission to "Go make disciples of all nations" (Matthew 28:19). The life of Christ as revealed through His followers has enabled multitudes to hear and believe the Good News so that today there are over two billion Christians around the world. In the next chapter, we'll discover what Christ's victory over death means to us practically and how we can face death without fear. God's plan for us is for abundant life. We will also look at several inspiring testimonies of those who have faced death with courage because of the strength of their faith in Christ.

Pray with me...

Lord, thank You that for my eternal blessing: You defeated death. Thank You for giving me the hope of everlasting life spent with You... a place of perfect joy. I do not need to be afraid of death any longer. You are my God and the One who sets free all those who suffer the uncertainty of what lies ahead. Your love has gone before me and opened up the way to my Heavenly Father. I am reconciled with God and have Your peace. Help me live with resurrection joy in my heart and carry Your hope to others who still suffer. Amen!

I am the resurrection and the life.
He who believes in me will live,
even though he dies;
and whoever lives and believes in me
will never die.
John 11:25-26

Chapter10

Abundant Life

No guilt in life, no fear in death —
This is the pow'r of Christ in me;
From life's first cry to final breath,
Jesus commands my destiny.
Keith Getty & Stuart Townsend
"In Christ Alone"

Our lives on earth are immortal until our work on earth is done.
George Whitefield

"A sovereign bullet." That's how Jim Bowers described the way that his wife and daughter were taken from this world. I remember the impact his remark made on me as I read his testimony in *The God You Can Trust* by Ray Pritchard. In the face of tragedy, can we trust God's sovereignty completely in our own lives and in the lives of our families? Jim and Roni were missionaries to Peru and in 2001 were mistakenly attacked by the military, which thought they were drug dealers. Bullets sprayed their plane, and what Jim called a sovereign bullet killed both his wife and infant daughter in the attack. Standing on his unshakeable faith Jim declared, "Nothing bad happened to them, they only got to heaven quicker than we did."[1] Would your faith be strong enough to enable you to make such a statement?

Life and death... we are surrounded with tragic events taking loved ones from us. Is death our enemy? Yes and no. In our last chapter we discussed that Jesus died for our sins, reconciled us to God by His shed blood, and overcame death as our final enemy. He proved this victory by His resurrection from the dead. Death has always been seen as an enemy until Christ opened the way to Heaven, into the glorious presence of our Eternal Father. Many followers of Christ over the past two thousand years have gone forth to their reward into eternity without fear of death, knowing they were going to their true home. The sting of death has been removed. Paul writes, "*'Where, O death, is your victory? Where, O death, is your sting?' The sting of death is sin, and the power of sin is the law. But thanks be to God! He gives us the victory through our Lord Jesus Christ*" (1 Corinthians 15:55-57).

Paul, the great apostle, knew what it was like to face death in his many years of serving Christ. As the first great missionary of the Christian faith, he did not fear death, and courageously faced opposition during many of his journeys. He suffered tremendous hostility from his fellow Jews and yet did not hold back from bringing the Good News into new lands.

> *We are pressed on every side by troubles, but we are not crushed. We are perplexed, but not driven to despair. We are hunted down, but never abandoned by God. We get knocked down, but we are not destroyed. Through suffering, our bodies continue to share in the death of Jesus so that the life of Jesus may also be seen in our bodies. Yes, we live under constant danger of death because we*

serve Jesus, so that the life of Jesus will be evident in our dying bodies. So we live in the face of death, but this has resulted in eternal life for you.

Corinthians 4:8-12 (NLT)

Why are those who serve Christ so wholeheartedly still subject to the trials and afflictions of this life? Shouldn't they have special protection keeping them from life's troubles as they minister in the name of Jesus? Doesn't it seem that there should be a special dispensation for those who do God's work. But over and over I have come upon testimonies of those who have suffered much in their work for the Lord. They suffered and brought God glory through their suffering. Again we can consider the incredible testimony of Paul, as he brought the Good News to Asia and explains that even in facing death, he understood God's purposes.

We think you ought to know, dear brothers and sisters, about the trouble we went through in the province of Asia. We were crushed and overwhelmed beyond our ability to endure, and we thought we would never live through it. In fact, we expected to die. But as a result, we stopped relying on ourselves and learned to rely only on God, who raises the dead. And he did rescue us from mortal danger, and he will rescue us again. We have placed our confidence in him, and he will continue to rescue us. And you are helping us by praying for us. Then many people will give thanks because God has graciously answered so many prayers for our safety.

2 Corinthians 1:8-11 (NLT)

Aren't these words encouraging to us in the midst of our trials and suffering? God does hear and answer prayer. The answer may not always be what we expect, but in faith we fix our eyes on Jesus and trust that our lives and the lives of our loved ones are in His hands. To those who face death without fear, Ray Pritchard states, "The world stands in awe of a suffering saint who clings to his faith in the midst of horrific circumstances. The world can partially counterfeit our joy, but it has no answer for the faith that shines the brightest in the darkest hours of the night."[2] *Out of Suffering Into Glory!*

The Promise of Abundant Life

Life is a gift from God. Each life is unique and every person has been made in the image of God. As a grandmother, I treasure my granddaughter, Lily, and her life is so very dear to me. Also precious are the sixty children in India in the Light Children's Home. At times theirs is a life versus death struggle. A number of these children are HIV positive, and some of them have had life threatening illnesses. Life is difficult in many countries of the world and death is very real to them. They suffer much and the promises of heaven, where there will be no more pain and sorrow but joy everlasting, have a special place in their hearts. We pray regularly for our own children and the children in India, that they would grow in the knowledge of God, that His grace would sustain them through suffering and hard times, and that they would experience fullness of life through Christ. This life in Christ is one of love, joy, and peace given by His Spirit regardless of our life circumstances.

God's desire is for all of us to experience fullness of life through a relationship with Jesus Christ. There is a difference between being alive as a member of the human race and being born again to live by the Spirit. Jesus spoke of this true life and warned of the one who seeks to destroy in the Gospel of John, *"The thief comes only to steal and kill and destroy; I have come that they may have life, and have it to the full"* (John 10:10). My pastor husband, Alan, first brought deeper meaning to the word "life" as used in John chapter 10 as he explained to me that there are two Greek words the Bible uses for life. One is "bio," from which we get biology, the study of living things. The other is "zoe," which we see used in the New Testament to describe that which is fully alive, eternally alive. It is the life we have **in Christ** who came to give true life. *"In Him we live and move and have our being"* (Acts 17:28). God's desire for you is to experience true life – abundant life. Life above the mundane. Life beyond the ordinary as we see our daily lives empowered by God's Spirit, refreshed by His Living Water, and touched by the grace of our Lord so we can fulfill our God-appointed destiny on earth.

One of the most powerful testimonies of the abundant life we have in Christ comes surprisingly from a man who suffered tragedy of Biblical proportions. Several years ago while teaching at a Christian conference center in New Hampshire, my husband and I heard Robert Rogers' story. During a flash flood in the Midwest he lost his wife and all four of his children. The amazing words you are about to read were given at a press conference only four days after the tragic event, and demonstrate the reality *out of suffering into glory*. His testimony also reflects one of the most significant truths from God's Word that *"All things work together for good"* (Romans 8:28).

> *This tragedy may have shattered my family, but it will not shatter my resolve to hope for good. We live in a fallen world. It rains on the just and the unjust alike. Evil seeks only to steal, kill and destroy, but God came that we might have life more abundantly. To honor the memory of my wife and children*

with something positive out of this terrible tragedy, please love, cherish, and savor your families every day. Hug and play with them. Eat meals and pray together, and tell your family you love them every day.... I'm not bitter against God. I've had a full, abundant life, and I'm fully persuaded that somehow by His grace, He will turn this tragedy into good. He has graced me with a blessed, abundant life. Now, He has given my wife and children a blessed and abundant life everlasting.

Although he was in great pain, Robert carried a peace that goes beyond understanding because of His faith in God's sovereignty. Many saw God's glory on him even in his suffering. What occurred in the weeks and months that followed brought Robert great comfort in his sorrow. *"God was being glorified and people's lives were being changed for the better through my family. It came at such a high cost. And yet God was already proving to me that He could indeed work all things for good, No matter how bad they might be."*[3] Today Robert is remarried and God has blessed him with children and a ministry through which he travels worldwide and shares his testimony. His ministry, Mighty in the Land, is dedicated to encouraging others to live a life for God with no regrets.

Choose Life...
for the Lord Is Your Life

While we are on earth you and I will suffer trials and face spiritual battles which will try to prevent us from experiencing life to the full. The battle is real, and we have an enemy whose desire is death and destruction. We see this around the world in wars, conflicts, and deeds done by evil men. In simplest terms it is the conflict between life and death. In my early days of walking with the Lord, I gained understanding of this as I studied the Old Testament book of Deuteronomy and spent time meditating on God's Word concerning life and death.

> *See, I set before you today* **life** *and prosperity,* **death** *and destruction. For I command you today to love the* LORD *your God, to walk in His ways, and to keep His commands, decrees and laws; then you will live and increase, and the* LORD *your God will bless you in the land you are entering to possess.*
>
> *But if your heart turns away and you are not obedient, and if you are drawn away to bow down to other gods and worship them, I declare to you this day that you will certainly be destroyed. You will not live long in the land you are crossing the Jordan to enter and possess.*
>
> *This day I call heaven and earth as witnesses against you that* **I have set before you life and death, blessings and curses**. *Now* **choose life**, *so that you and your children may live, and that you may love the Lord your God, listen to His voice, and hold fast to Him.* **For the Lord is your life.**
>
> Deuteronomy 30:15-20

Readers, life gives us many choices. Many of the choices involve obeying and listening to our God-given conscience. You may remember not so wise choices you made in your childhood, which resulted in certain consequences—perhaps not so pleasant ones. I had a lot of those consequences affect my childhood, and there was resulting pain from disobeying God's commandments. According to the Deuteronomy passage, the Lord asks of us, *"to love the Lord your God, to walk in His ways, and to keep His commands."* How much do you love the Lord? With all your heart, soul, mind and strength? Do you walk in His ways? Do you keep His commands? Unfortunately today very few people on the street could recite the Ten Commandments. Could you?

However, as New Testament followers of God, we have it so much easier. Jesus told us that the two most important command-ments are to, *"Love the Lord your God with all your heart and with all your soul and with all your mind and with all your strength. The second is this: 'Love your neighbor as yourself.' There is no command-ment greater than these"* (Mark 12:30-31). God is love and He is your life. To live in love is to live the life God has purposed for us as sons and daughters made in His image. This is the way of true life, of "zoe," which is a part of the abundant life Jesus promised. One of the greatest joys in life is to be used as an ambassador of the Kingdom of Love, sharing God's love with people you encounter on a daily basis. So many around us are hurting or have lost their way. Paul gives us this encouragement from God's Word. *"Be imi-tators of God, therefore, as dearly loved children, and live a life of love"* (Ephesians 5:1a).

Millions around the world today are suffering because of wrong choices. Many are blinded to the glorious reality of the One True God and Jesus Christ the Savior and do not love Him or walk in His ways or keep His commands. They suffer the consequences of choosing to serve gods that are not gods but are instead cruel masters of enslavement—drugs, alcohol, sex, pornography, materi-alism, gambling, food addiction, and wrong soul ties. Others seek power, position, pleasure, and prestige and spend their lives in wasted pursuits of that which will never satisfy. If only they would turn from sin, confess their wrongdoing, accept Christ as Savior, and trust in His power to change their lives, then they would come to know the true life found in Jesus. And they would know the greatest love, which alone fills the deepest reservoir of man's soul, and drink from the fountain of His life.

> *Your love, O LORD, reaches to the heavens, your faithfulness to the skies. Your righteousness is like the mighty mountains, your justice like the great deep. O LORD, you preserve both man and beast. How priceless is your unfailing love! Both high and low among men find refuge in the shadow of your wings. They feast on the abundance of your house; you give them drink from your river of delights. For with you is the* **fountain of life.**

> Psalm 36:5-9

Knowing God is knowing true life. *"Now* **choose life***, so that you and your children may live, and that you may love the Lord your God, listen to his voice, and hold fast to him.* **For the Lord is your life"** (Deuteronomy 30:19b-20a). Abundant life, everlasting life, true life, the wellspring of life, the river of life, life overflowing, life to the full—it's all found in Jesus Christ. He revealed Himself while on earth as the *"Bread of Life,"* (John 6:35) and *"the Way, the Truth, and the Life"* (John 14:6). For no one comes to the Father, except through Him. And He has given us the gift of the Holy Spirit to teach us His ways and guide us in life. *"The Spirit gives life; the flesh counts for nothing. The words I have spoken to you are spirit and they are life"* (John 6:63). Aren't you grateful for the presence of the Holy Spirit who is the helper, revealer of truth, encourager, and comforter to all who trust in Him?

We all live in this world in very fragile earth-suits, and before us is the certainty of death. But whether or not we face death courageously and without fear depends on our intimate relationship with God. When we traveled to India in 2010 for our first mission trip to visit the Light Children's Home I had no fear. My sister was nervous that we were going to India. She had read of terrible persecution against Christians in the Orissa region of India where extremists had burned churches and killed Christians. But when you are in God's will, doing God's work, you do not need to fear death. Remember the quote I shared at the beginning of this chapter, *"We are immortal until our work on earth is done"* (George Whitefield).

Along the same lines, I never tire of reflecting on these words of Paul, one of my great heroes from the Bible. He declared,

> *I eagerly expect and hope that I will in no way be ashamed, but will have sufficient courage so that now as always Christ will be exalted in my body, whether by life or by death. **For to me, to live is Christ and to die is gain**. If I am to go on living in the body, this will mean fruitful labor for me. Yet what shall I choose? I do not know! I am torn between the two: I desire to depart and be with Christ, which is better by far; but it is more necessary for you that I remain in the body. Convinced of this, I know that I will remain, and I will continue with all of you for your progress and joy in the faith, so that through my being with you again your joy in Christ Jesus will overflow on account of me.*

> Philippians 1:20-26

Flight to Heaven

For Christians, death is the commencement of our real life with the Lord in our heavenly home. Paul states this is *"far better."* My husband and I recently finished reading *Flight to Heaven*, a book describing a young pilot's experience during his near-death encounter. Dale Black was the only survivor of a small plane, which crashed in 1969 in the suburbs of southern California. His account of visiting a magnificent heavenly city while hospitalized in a life and death struggle to survive almost defies description.

> *The entire city was bathed in light, an opaque whiteness in which the light was intense but diffused. In that dazzling light every color imaginable seemed to exist and...if joy could be given colors, they would be these colors...pure and innocent, like children playing in a fountain, splashing, chasing each other, gurgling with laughter. Water everywhere sparkled in the sunshine.... Somehow I knew that light and life and love were connected and interrelated. It was as if the very heart of God lay open for everyone in heaven to bask in its glory, to warm themselves in its presence, to bathe in its almost liquid properties so they could be restored, renewed, and refreshed.[4]*

God has breathed His breath into you. His breath keeps you alive. Before you is eternal life. On earth He wants to bless you with abundant life, life to the full. He asks you to choose to love Him, to walk in His ways, to seek Him, and to allow His Spirit to reveal true life to you. Life lived from the source of life—God our Father, Jesus our Redeemer, His Spirit our teacher. You are not alone in this life. In any trial or suffering, He is with you. Every word I have shared with you in this book has been shared with this desire from my heart, *"these are written that you may believe that Jesus is the Christ, the Son of God, and that by believing you may have **life** in his name"* (John 20:31).

Pray with me...

Father, give me Your life, the true life found in Christ. I want to know You and trust You and believe in You more each day. Walk with me each day and help me to keep my eyes fixed on the goal of everlasting life. This world is not my true home. This world will pass away, but You have a home waiting for me where I will see You face to face and be reunited with my loved ones who have gone before me. I thank You Lord for all You have done for me. I love You Jesus and surrender again all my hopes, dreams, and desires so that Your perfect will would be done in my life. I also give You all my suffering for Your redemptive purposes. I don't want my sorrows to be wasted. Use for good all that has been allowed in my life. And may I give You all the glory now and forever. Amen!

I have come that they may have life,
and that they may have it more abundantly.

John 10:10

Chapter 11

Glory Revealed

*I consider that our present sufferings
are not worth comparing
with the glory that will be revealed in us.*
Romans 8:18

*Jesus did not come to explain away suffering
or remove it.
He came to fill it with His presence.*
Paul Claudel

The journey of suffering which we will all travel on for some part of our life may seem long, but in view of eternity, it will soon transition to the joy of God's glory revealed in us and to us. It was what we saw in the life of our Savior Jesus as He was obedient to fulfill the Father's plan of redemption. This plan culminated in His suffering on the cross, revealing the great love of God our Father. Remember what made this possible? *"For the joy set before Him, He endured the cross"* (Hebrews 12:2). We too have the promise of joy — Jesus Himself is our joy regardless of the circumstances which surround us at present. In following the life of Jesus in His sufferings, we witnessed the glorious joy of His beloved follow-ers in seeing the risen Christ. His suffering passed — it was limited. And so, we too are told that our suffering will pass. For many years these words of Paul, which he shared with believers struggling in Corinth, have encouraged my spirit: *"For our light and momentary troubles are achieving for us an eternal glory that far outweighs them all. So we fix our eyes not on what is seen, but on what is unseen. For what is seen is temporary, but what is unseen is eternal"* (2 Corinthians 4:17-17). Eternal glory awaits you, dear reader!

The glory of God is the prize set before us. This world will pass; it is temporary and our trials are limited. But His glory is eternal and we must fix our eyes on it. My husband and I are now in the autumn of life. Winter isn't too far ahead. Heaven seems more and more real to us in the midst of the challenges of aging. Praise God! There is an end to suffering and there is a glorious place awaiting us. One day we shall experience our God in all His glory and splendor. For a number of years I have been reflecting and teaching on the glory of God. One of my favorite passages I quote is from the prophet Isaiah.

> *Arise, shine, for your light has come, and the glory of the* LORD
> *rises upon you. See, darkness covers the earth*
> *and thick darkness is over the peoples,*
> *but the* LORD *rises upon you and his glory appears over you.*
>
> *The sun will no more be your light by day, nor will the bright-ness of the moon shine on you, for the* LORD *will be your ever-lasting light, and your God will be your glory.*
> *Your sun will never set again, and your moon will wane no more;*
> *the* LORD *will be your everlasting light,*
> *and your days of sorrow will end.*

Isaiah 60:1-2, 19-20

This passage tells us that one day, *"God will be your glory"* and *"your days of sorrow will end."* Let's long for that day when we will see and experience His glory. How do we describe God's glory? It is seen in His light and joy which overcome all darkness and sorrow. It's also the radiance, the brilliance, the perfection, and wonder of God manifesting Himself to His creation in purple mountain grandeur, a brilliant sunrise, and the infinity of stars on a cloudless night. We see His glory in the revelation of God that touches our lives each day enabling us to know Him better as we seek Him above all else. It is also revealed to us — Spirit to spirit — as we worship Him in the beauty of His holiness, humbly acknowledging He is everything to us. Life... breath... hope... love... goodness... truth... peace... joy... satisfaction. How incredible that from the time of creation, God intended to share His glory with man! *"What is man that you are mindful of him, the son of man that you care for him? You made him a little lower than the heavenly beings and crowned him with glory and honor"* (Psalm 8:4-5). Sin tarnished the glory of God in man and brought pain and suffering into this world through one man. Yet, another man, the sinless Son of God, in His supreme act of redemptive suffering, restored man to the glory of God. Now we may know a foretaste of the glory we will one day share in Heaven when we allow His plans and purposes to be realized in our suffering. For you and I also experience redemptive suffering as we surrender to God's will in our trials, in our pain, in our afflictions. *"I consider that our present sufferings are not worth comparing with the glory that will be revealed in us"* (Romans 8:18). For we are heirs of God and co-heirs with Christ and we share in His glory as we participate in His sufferings while on earth (Romans 8:17).

In Your Suffering Bless Others

His glory revealed in and through our lives means we live differently now than we did before. His love and His Spirit abide in us. You are Christ's hands and feet and heart in this world. Are you on a daily basis living to reflect His glory to those around you, by acting as Jesus would in this world? Are you — in spite of your trials and suffering — seeking ways to help alleviate the suffering around you? Ask God to show you how you can make a difference in the lives of those you know and those you meet. Remember what Jesus told His followers. *"Let your light shine before men, that they may see your good deeds and praise your Father in heaven"* (Matthew 5:6).

Think of the chapters you just read. Pray that God would show you ways to bring the Bread of Life to the hungry — both literally and spiritually. Know God's Word, have it stored in your heart so that you can speak it to those starving for truth. Minister to the thirsty with the gift of the water of life — eternal life through Jesus. Share that God's Spirit is ready to be poured out to those who feel they're in a desert time. Comfort the grieving with your presence, offering the hope you have found in Christ. Go to those who feel rejected and despised. Let them know you care and will be their friend. Pray for the sick. Be bold. Jesus told His followers that those who believe *"will place their hands on sick people and they will get well"* (Mark 16:18). Sometimes faith is spelled R-I-S-K, but your faith pleases God. And prayer always touches heaven to release God's presence. In my new boldness over the last few years, I have offered prayer to people in public places, and 99% accept and are grateful for prayer.

Also seek God's guidance in how to minister His love to those who have been deserted, forsaken, or abandoned — like single parents, divorced friends, and neglected, abused, or orphaned children. So many around us are hurting and your suffering has equipped you to know that the answer to the greatest sorrow is in knowing the One who suffered for us and is now with us. Our Savior has said, *"never will I leave you; never will I forsake you"* (Hebrews 13:5). He is the same God who tells us that yes, we will have trouble in this world; yes, there will be fearful events. But He declares, *"Don't be afraid; just believe"* (Mark 5:36). I love those five powerful words. With them you can master your own fears and walk in this world fearlessly, bringing the peace of Christ to those who are anxious and distressed, the peace which *"transcends all understanding"* (Philippians 4:7). (See Appendix for additional verses to help overcome fear and anxiety.)

Know the ABC's of Salvation

For those you know who are facing death through terminal illness or are in the autumn of life, be genuine and express your certainty that they can absolutely know where they are going when they die. Share with them that Jesus invites them into fellowship and desires that their name be written in the Book of Life. Know the ABC's of Salvation to be able to lead them to Christ.

Admit: Confess to God that you are a sinner. Repent or turn away from your sin.

Believe: Trust that Jesus is God's Son and He came to save people from their sins.

Commit: Give your life to Jesus. Ask Him to be your Lord and Savior.

Something amazing happens in heaven when someone comes to know Jesus Christ as Savior. *"I tell you, there is rejoicing in the presence of the angels of God over one sinner who repents"* (Luke 15:10). You will participate in the glory of God in seeing grace abound to one who opens his or her heart to Christ in their greatest time of need. Do not hold back with loved ones or friends approaching death, let the Spirit of God guide you to be a part of one of the most important things you will ever do on earth…. introducing someone to Jesus, the Redeemer.

Out of Suffering Into Glory was given to me by the Lord as the title and theme of this book. I know that I would not have been writing this book had it not been for my years of suffering emotional pain in childhood. In recent years some of it has resurfaced, along with troubles from serious food intolerances, digestive issues, and chronic fatigue. Yet in my own situation, I <u>still</u> know the joy of the Lord in my innermost being. My God <u>does</u> meet my deepest needs. I <u>am</u> content in knowing Christ as my greatest treasure. And His Spirit reveals God's abundant life within me. My trials have enabled me in some measure to feel the suffering of my brothers and sisters around the world, especially those in India who suffer with leprosy. As I shared with them the message from which this book developed, I experienced the taste of God's glory as His presence was powerfully manifested in that simple church in rural India. "Jesus knows your suffering," I told them. "He also suffered greatly on earth and knows what it is like to be hungry, thirsty, rejected, in pain and anguish, and facing death. He experienced it for you and for me. He loves you and is a great and loving God worthy of your devotion." I knew God was pouring out His love and grace upon those gathered in that humble room as they turned to Him in worship and tasted His glory.

The reality of God's Word was revealed to them—in Him we are set free and made whole. *"But whenever anyone turns to the Lord, the veil is taken away. Now the Lord is the Spirit, and where the Spirit of the Lord is, there is freedom. And we, who with unveiled faces all reflect the Lord's glory, are being transformed into his likeness with ever-increasing glory, which comes from the Lord, who is the Spirit"* (2 Corinthians 3:16-18). In that room in India many turned to the Lord and knew at that moment freedom from pain, rejection, hunger, fear, and hopelessness. Through brokenness we are changed into His likeness. You and I, even in our suffering, have been given the privilege of carrying the treasure of His glory in these frail, earthen vessels. For many of us it is the brokenness of our lives that allows the hidden beauty of Christ to be seen. In *Don't Waste Your Sorrows*, author Paul Billheimer writes, "There is no way that Christ-like character can be formed in man without brokenness, for without it, he will remain hard, self-centered, unbroken, and therefore un-Christlike. Whole, unbruised, unbroken people are of little use to God."[1]

But rejoice! There is hope in the Lord. Remember suffering is not without purpose. Ultimately it is suffering and trials which lead many of us to God and enable His love to be revealed to us. From the hardened criminal who finds Christ in his jail cell, to the prodigal who has traveled on all the wrong paths seeking pleasure, to the philosopher who has nowhere else to turn at the end of his intellectual pursuits, to the rich man who never has enough money... only one treasure will satisfy them all. These and multitudes of others have had their hearts return to their Creator in acknowledgement that there is nowhere else to look for meaning and love. Only through Christ do we find hope and fulfillment for our souls. His love meets every need. *"And we rejoice in the hope of the glory of God.*

Not only so, but we also rejoice in our sufferings, because we know that suffering produces perseverance; perseverance, character; and character, hope. And hope does not disappoint us, because God has poured out his love into our hearts by the Holy Spirit, whom he has given us" (Romans 5:2b-5). Rejoice, dear friends. His Spirit is pouring God's love daily into your hearts. Receive it as refreshment for your soul.

Find Solace in Jesus

As I have continued to meditate on suffering and glory, the Holy Spirit showed me two visions. In one there was the awareness of deliverance from suffering (both in an earthly reality and in a spiritual sense) by having before us the loving arms of our Savior, the King of Glory. My soul felt overjoyed with the vision of coming out of suffering, as one would be freed from a dark, oppressive place, and then going into the light of God's Love and Glory as His embrace encompassed me. In that embrace was the realm of His Glory where suffering has been redeemed and where there is no more pain or sorrow. It is the place where nothing will ever separate us from God's love found in Christ Jesus.

Jesus Himself IS the answer to all suffering. He is truly the only Savior for mankind. His suffering and resurrection have made known to us that *"God so loved the world that he gave his one and only Son, that whoever believes in him shall not perish but have eternal life. For God did not send his Son into the world to condemn the world, but to save the world through him"* (John 3:16-17). His love rescues, redeems, and makes whole. Respond to His love in sincere worship, in humble surrender, and in whole-hearted devotion. In the last days the world is seeing the revelation of God like never before.

People around the world are having dreams and visions of Jesus Christ. This relates to the second vision I saw of a tsunami wave covering the earth. In contrast to a physical tsunami which brings destruction, the one I saw was a spiritual wave of Life bringing the Glory of God to the earth. *"For the earth will be filled with the knowledge of the Glory of the Lord, as the waters cover the sea"* (Isaiah 2:13). Pour out Your Glory God! The earth is thirsting for the Glory and presence of God. Dear reader, yearn for His presence. It is where you will experience His Glory and receive life's greatest blessings for your soul. Brenton Brown writes,

> *In the glory of Your presence,*
> *I find rest for my soul*
> *In the depths of Your love,*
> *I find peace makes me whole*
> *I love, I love, I love Your presence ...*
> *I love, I love, I love You Jesus*

As I was coming to the end of writing *Out of Suffering Into Glory*, I was encouraged to read online from author Lee Strobel what I share as a confirmation of the truth that God is Emanuel, God with us. His presence may not take away your suffering but He will redeem it. Jesus suffered but is now in Glory. Strobel writes of our all-sufficient Savior's ability to sympathize perfectly with us in our present needs.

> *God's ultimate answer to suffering isn't an explanation; it's the incarnation. Suffering is a personal problem; it demands a personal response. And God isn't some distant, detached, and disinterested deity; He entered into our world and personally experienced our pain. Jesus is there in the lowest places of our lives. Are you broken? He was broken, like bread, for us. Are you*

despised? He was despised and rejected of men. Do you cry out that you can't take any more? He was a man of sorrows and acquainted with grief. Did someone betray you? He was sold out. Are your most tender relationships broken? He loved and He was rejected. Did people turn from you? They hid their faces from Him as if He were a leper. Does He descend into all of our hells? Yes, He does. From the depths of a Nazi death camp, Corrie ten Boom wrote these words: "No matter how deep our darkness, He is deeper still." Every tear we shed becomes his tear.[2]

I don't know the journey of your suffering, but God knows. Our ways are known to Him. We do not know the number of days allotted to us on earth, but He knows. What we can be certain of is where we will spend eternity. You can also be assured that you are never alone, that the gift of His Spirit abides in you. Trust in His Word and in the incredible promises given to strengthen you daily. You were made to fellowship with God, to grow in intimacy with your Lord and Savior, to know that you are never without hope in Him. Live in humility and dependence on God and trust always that *"in ALL things God works for the good of those who love him, who have been called according to his purpose"* (Romans 8:28).

Dear friend, know that you were in my mind as I wrote this book. I love you and pray that you have encountered God in a new and powerful way as you have read. I truly believe God will use for good every trial and suffering that you experience in your life. And His will is that you know Him in His Glory and grace. In closing, I share these precious words God gave me for you…

Arise, shine for Your Light has come. Yes, your enemy has sent pain and trials your way. But rise up in My strength. Rise up as overcomers. Let My Light lead you and guide you along paths of righteousness, let My goodness touch your life, hope in Me and you will be lifted up. Trust Me and I will uphold you. Keep your eyes on Me and you will not fall. Let Me send My Spirit and power into your life to strengthen you. I am coming in power. I am coming to the earth to reveal My Glory. Children of God, arise, and come into your rightful place, put off grave clothes, put off every weight and sin, put off darkness that remains hidden in inner places of your life. Let My light consume you and transform you. I am coming for a radiant church. I am coming for My bride. My love is bursting forth upon her, and My people are being gathered to do My will and further My Kingdom. Seek My face. Seek My presence. Turn from the world and spend time in the secret place of My heart. You are My beloved. I am with you always.

To the only God our Savior be glory, majesty, power and authority,
through Jesus Christ our Lord, before all ages,
now and forevermore! Amen.

Jude 25

OUT OF SUFFERING INTO GLORY!

Appendix

God's Redemptive Purposes For Suffering

In our suffering we recognize our need for God.

Psalm 118:5

In our suffering we identify with the suffering of Jesus Christ.

Romans 8:17

In our suffering pride and self-sufficiency are overcome and we are humbled.

Psalm 107:39

In our suffering we repent of all that prevents us from knowing God's purposes.

Job 42:1-6

In our suffering our faith is proved genuine and strengthened.

1 Peter 1:6-7

In our suffering new truths about God are revealed to us by the Holy Spirit.

John 16:13-14

In our suffering we grow in our empathy and compassion for others who suffer.

2 Corinthians 1:5

In our suffering and weakness we understand the complete sufficiency of God's grace.

2 Corinthians 12:9-10

In our suffering God's comfort comes to us and we learn how to comfort and care for others.

2 Corinthians 1:3-7

In our suffering we discover ministries we might never have realized.

Philippians 1:12

In our suffering we have the privilege to share the Gospel.

2 Timothy 2:8-10

In our suffering our character is matured into Christ-likeness.

Romans 5:3-5

In our suffering God's promises and the hope of heaven become real.

Psalm 119:50

In our suffering we are given the honor to bring God glory.

1 Peter 1:7

In our suffering we look to the day when we shall see our Redeemer face to face.

Job. 19:25-27

26 Blessings From God's Word

Answered Prayer "If you abide in Me, and My words abide in you, you will ask what you desire, and it shall be done for you." John 15:7

Blessing "Blessed is the man who does not walk in the counsel of the wicked or stand in the way of sinners or sit in the seat of mockers. But his delight is in the law of the LORD, and on His law he meditates day and night. He is like a tree planted by streams of water, which yields its fruit in season and whose leaf does not wither. Whatever he does prospers." Psalm 1:13

Cleansing "You are already clean because of the word I have spoken to you." John 15:3 "...as Christ loved the church and gave himself up for her to make her holy, cleansing her by the washing with water through the word, and to present her to Himself as a radiant church, without stain or wrinkle or any other blemish, but holy and blameless." Ephesians 5:25-27

Delight "I delight in Your decrees; I will not neglect Your word." "Your statutes are my delight; they are my counselors." "Direct me in the path of Your commands, for there I find delight." Psalm 119:16, 24, 35

Encouragement "For everything that was written in the past was written to teach us, so that through endurance and the encouragement of the Scriptures we might have hope." Romans 15:4

Faith "So then faith comes by hearing, and hearing by the word of God." Romans 10:17

Guidance "Your word is a lamp to my feet and a light to my path." Psalm 119:105

Hope "My soul faints with longing for Your salvation, but I have put my hope in Your word." Psalm 119:81

Instruction "All Scripture is given by inspiration of God, and is profitable for doctrine, for reproof, for correction, for instruction in righteousness, that the man of God may be complete, thoroughly equipped for every good work." 2 Timothy 3:16-17

Joy "If you obey My commands, you will remain in My love, just as I have obeyed My Father's commands and remain in His love. I have told you this so that My joy may be in you and that your joy may be complete." John 15:10-11 "Your statutes are my heritage forever; they are the joy of my heart." Psalm 119:111

Knowledge "My son, if you receive My words, and treasure My commands within you, so that you incline your ear to wisdom, and apply your heart to understanding; Yes, if you cry out for discernment, and lift up your voice for understanding; If you seek her as silver, and search for her as for hidden treasures; Then you will understand the fear of the LORD, and find the knowledge of God." Proverbs 2:1-5

Life "In the beginning was the Word, and the Word was with God, and the Word was God. He was in the beginning with God. All things were made through Him, and without Him nothing was made that was made. In Him was life, and the life was the light of men." John 1:1-4

Meditation "Do not let this Book of the Law depart from your mouth; meditate on it day and night, so that you may be careful to do everything written in it. Then you will be prosperous and successful." Joshua 1:8

New Heart and New Spirit "I will give you a new heart and put a new spirit in you; I will remove from you your heart of stone and give you a heart of flesh. And I will put My Spirit in you and move you to follow My decrees and be careful to keep My laws." Ezekiel 36:26-27

Obedience "Before I was afflicted I went astray, but now I obey Your word... I have kept my feet from every evil path so that I might obey Your word... Your statutes are wonderful; therefore I obey them." Psalm 119:67,101, 129

Purity "How can a young man keep his way pure? By living according to Your word." Psalm 119:9

Quickening "For the word of God is living and powerful, and sharper than any two-edged sword, piercing even to the division of soul and spirit, and of joints and marrow, and is a discerner of the thoughts and intents of the heart." Hebrews 4:12

Rebirth "For you have been born again, not of perishable seed, but of imperishable, through the living and enduring word of God." 1 Peter 1:23

Sword of the Spirit "In addition to all this, take up the shield of faith, with which you can extinguish all the flaming arrows of the evil one. Take the helmet of salvation and the sword of the Spirit, which is the word of God." Ephesians 6:16-17

Truth "Sanctify them by the truth; Your word is truth." John 17:17

Understanding "The unfolding of Your words gives light; it gives understanding to the simple... May my cry come before You, O LORD; give me understanding according to Your word." Psalm 119:30,169

Victory over temptation "Then Jesus was led by the Spirit into the desert to be tempted by the devil. After fasting forty days and forty nights, He was hungry. The tempter came to Him and said, "If you are the Son of God, tell these stones to become bread." Jesus answered, "It is written: 'Man does not live on bread alone, but on every word that comes from the mouth of God.'" Matthew 4:1-4

Wisdom "Let the Word of Christ dwell in you richly as you teach and admonish one another with all wisdom, and as you sing psalms, hymns and spiritual songs with gratitude in your hearts to God." Colossians 3:16

eXamination "For the word of God is living and powerful, and sharper than any two-edged sword, piercing even to the division of soul and spirit, and of joints and marrow, and is a discerner of the thoughts and intents of the heart." Hebrews 4:12

Years "My son, do not forget My teaching, but keep My commands in your heart, for they will prolong your life many years and bring you prosperity." Proverbs 3:1-2

Zeal "My zeal wears me out, for my enemies ignore your words." Psalm 119:139

Scripture Prayer Guides

*Verses to use during your personal prayer time
in meditation, intercession and thanksgiving.*

Promises On
Endurance

For you have been born again, not of perishable seed, but of imperishable, through the living and ENDURING word of God. For, "All men are like grass, and all their glory is like the flowers of the field; the grass withers and the flowers fall, but the word of the Lord stands forever."

1 Peter 1: 23-25

For everything that was written in the past was written to teach us, so that through ENDURANCE and the encouragement of the Scriptures we might have hope. May the God who gives ENDURANCE and encouragement give you a spirit of unity among yourselves as you follow Christ Jesus, so that with one heart and mouth you may glorify the God and Father of our Lord Jesus Christ.

Romans 15:4-6

May His name ENDURE forever; may it continue as long as the sun. All nations will be blessed through Him, and they will call Him blessed.

Psalm 72:17

I know that everything God does will ENDURE forever; nothing can be added to it and nothing taken from it. God does it so that men will revere Him.

Ecclesiastes 3:14

Let us fix our eyes on Jesus, the author and perfecter of our faith, who for the joy set before Him ENDURED the cross, scorning its shame, and sat down at the right hand of the throne of God. Consider Him who ENDURED such opposition from sinful men, so that you will not grow weary and lose heart.

Hebrews 12:2-3

ENDURE hardship as discipline; God is treating you as sons. For what son is not disciplined by his father? Our fathers disciplined us for a little while as they thought best; but God disciplines us for our good, that we may share in His holiness.

Hebrews 12:7, 10

This calls for patient ENDURANCE on the part of the saints who obey God's commandments and remain faithful to Jesus.

Revelation 14:12

Here is a trustworthy saying: If we died with Him, we will also live with Him; if we ENDURE, we will also reign with Him.

2 Timothy 2:11-12

Give thanks to the LORD, for He is good.
His love endures forever.
Psalm 136:1

Promises On
Overcoming Fear

God is our refuge and strength, an ever-present help in trouble. Therefore we will not fear, though the earth give way, and the mountains fall into the heart of the sea.

Psalms 46:1-2

The Lord is my light and my salvation – whom shall I fear? The Lord is the stronghold of my life – of whom shall I be afraid? … Though an army besiege me, my heart will not fear; though war break out against me, even then will I be confident.

Psalm 27:3

Do not fear for I am with you. Do not be dismayed for I am your God. I will strengthen you, and help you. I will uphold you with my righteous right hand.

Isaiah 41:10

In my anguish I cried to the Lord and He answered by setting me free. The Lord is with me; I will not be afraid. What can man do to me?

Psalm 118:5

When I am afraid, I will trust in You. In God whose word I praise, in God I trust. I will not be afraid.

Psalm 56:3

Have mercy on me, O God, have mercy on me. For in You my soul takes refuge. I will take refuge in the shadow of Your wings until the disaster has passed.

Psalm 57:1

Strengthen the feeble hands, steady the knees that give way; say to those with fearful hearts, "Be strong, do not fear," Your God will come to save you.

Isaiah 35:3-4

For God has not given us the spirit of fear; but of power, and of love, and of a sound mind.

2 Timothy 1:7

There is no fear in love. But perfect love drives out fear, because fear has to do with punishment. The one who fears is not made perfect in love.

1 John 4:18

The Lord is my Shepherd, I shall not want....
Even though I walk through the valley of the shadow of death,
I will fear no evil, for You are with me.
Your rod and Your staff, they comfort me.
You prepare a table before me
in the presence of my enemies.
You anoint my head with oil; my cup overflows. Surely
goodness and love will follow me
all the days of my life,
and I will dwell in the house of the Lord forever.

Psalm 23

Promises On
God's Love

For God so LOVED the world that He gave his One and only Son, that whoever believes in Him shall not perish but have eternal life. For God did not send His Son into the world to condemn the world, but to save the world through Him.

John 3:16-17

For as high as the heavens are above the earth, so great is His LOVE for those who fear Him; as far as the east is from the west, so far has He removed our transgressions from us.

Psalm 103:11-12

For the word of the Lord is right and true; He is faithful in all He does. The Lord loves righteousness and justice; the earth is full of his unfailing LOVE... We wait in hope for the Lord; He is our help and our shield. In Him our hearts rejoice, for we trust in His holy name.

Psalm 33:4-5, 21-22

Know therefore that the Lord your God is God; He is the faithful God, keeping His covenant of love to a thousand generations of those who love Him and keep His commands.

Deuteronomy 7:9

As the Father has loved Me, so have I LOVED you. Now remain in My LOVE. My command is this: Love each other as I have LOVED you. Greater LOVE has no one than this - that he lay down his life for his friends.

John 15:9,12-13

How great is the LOVE the Father has lavished on us, that we should be called children of God! And that is what we are!

1 John 3:1

This is how God showed His LOVE among us: He sent His one and only Son into the world that we might live through Him. This is LOVE: not that we loved God, but that He LOVED us and sent His Son as an atoning sacrifice for our sins.

1 John 4:9-10

God is LOVE. Whoever lives in love lives in God, and God in him. In this way, LOVE is made complete among us so that we will have confidence on the day of judgment, because in this world we are like Him. There is no fear in love. But perfect love drives out fear.

1 John 4:16b

For I am convinced that neither death nor life, neither angels nor demons, neither the present nor the future, nor any powers, neither height nor depth, nor anything else in all creation, will be able to separate us from the love of God that is in Christ Jesus our Lord.
Romans 8:38-39

Promises On

Grace

The Word became flesh and made His dwelling among us. We have seen His glory, the glory of the One and Only, who came from the Father, full of GRACE and truth.

John 1:14

For the GRACE of God that brings salvation has appeared to all men. It teaches us to say "No" to ungodliness and worldly passions, and to live self-controlled, upright and godly lives in this present age, while we wait for the blessed hope — the glorious appearing of our great God and Savior, Jesus Christ, who gave Himself for us to redeem us from all wickedness and to purify for Himself a people that are His very own, eager to do what is good.

Titus 2: 11-14

How much more will those who receive God's abundant provision of GRACE and of the gift of righteousness reign in life through the one man, Jesus Christ.

Romans 5:17

And God is able to make all GRACE abound to you, so that in all things at all times, having all that you need, you will abound in every good work.

2 Corinthians 9:8

But because of His great love for us, God, who is rich in mercy, made us alive with Christ even when we were dead in transgressions — it is by GRACE you have been saved.

Ephesians 2:4-5

For it is by GRACE you have been saved, through faith — and this not from yourselves, it is the gift of God — not by works, so that no one can boast. For we are God's workmanship, created in Christ Jesus to do good works, which God prepared in advance for us to do.

Ephesians 2:8-10

Paul: But He said to me, "My GRACE is sufficient for you, for My power is made perfect in weakness. That is why, for Christ's sake, I delight in weaknesses, in insults, in hardships, in persecutions, in difficulties. For when I am weak, then I am strong."

2 Corinthians 12:9-10

GOD'S RICHES AT CHRIST'S EXPENSE

"Grace is the sum of all blessings
that come from God through Christ.
Grace is God's forgiving disposition
toward mankind as weak, guilty and lost.
God provided grace, and Christ personified it."
Herbert Lockyer

Promises On

Healing

Praise the LORD, O my soul; all my inmost being, praise His holy name. Praise the LORD, O my soul, and forget not all His bene-fits — who forgives all your sins and HEALS all your diseases, who redeems your life from the pit and crowns you with love and com-passion, who satisfies your desires with good things so that your youth is renewed like the eagle's.

Psalm 103:1-5

But He was pierced for our transgressions, He was crushed for our iniquities; the punishment that brought us peace was upon Him, and by His wounds we are HEALED.

Isaiah 53:5

He said, "If you listen carefully to the voice of the LORD your God and do what is right in his eyes, if you pay attention to his commands and keep all his decrees, I will not bring on you any of the diseases I brought on the Egyptians, for I am the LORD, who HEALS you."

Exodus 15:26

HEAL me, O LORD, and I will be HEALED; save me and I will be saved, for You are the one I praise.

Jeremiah 17:14

When Jesus landed and saw a large crowd, He had compassion on them and HEALED their sick. ... And when the men of that place recognized Jesus, they sent word to all the surrounding country. People brought all their sick to Him, and begged Him to let the sick just touch the edge of His cloak, and all who touched Him were HEALED.

Matthew 14:14,35-36

My son, pay attention to what I say; listen closely to My words. Do not let them out of your sight, keep them within your heart; for they are life to those who find them and HEALTH to a man's whole body.

Proverbs 4:20-22

I am troubled; O Lord, come to my aid! But what can I say? He has spoken to me, and He Himself has done this. I will walk humbly all my years because of this anguish of my soul. Lord, by such things men live; and my spirit finds life in them too. You restored me to HEALTH and let me live. Surely it was for my benefit that I suffered such anguish.

Isaiah 38:14b-17

Dear friend, I pray that you may enjoy good health and
that all may go well with you,
even as your soul is getting along well.
3 John 2

Promises On

Joy

Behold, I bring you good news of great JOY that will be for all people. For to you this day is born a Savior who is Christ the Lord.

Luke 2:10-11

REJOICE in the Lord always. I will say it again: REJOICE! Let your gentleness be evident to all. The Lord is near. Do not be anxious about anything,

Philippians 4:4-6a

In this you greatly REJOICE, though now for a little while you may have had to suffer grief in all kinds of trials. These have come so that your faith—of greater worth than gold, which perishes even though refined by fire—may be proved genuine and may result in praise, glory and honor when Jesus Christ is revealed.

1 Peter 1:6-7

Though you have not seen Him, you love Him; and even though you do not see Him now, you believe in Him and are filled with an inexpressible and glorious JOY.

1 Peter 1:8

In Your presence is fullness of JOY, eternal pleasures at Your right hand.

Psalm 16:11

Weeping may endure for a night, but JOY comes in the morning.

Psalm 30:5b

You satisfy us with Your unfailing love, that we may sing for JOY and be glad all our days.

Psalm 50:14

[Though my life suffers the loss of all things] YET I will REJOICE in the Lord, I will be JOYFUL in God my Savior. The Sovereign Lord is my strength; He makes my feet like the feet of the deer, He enables me to go to the heights.

Habakkuk 3:17-19

There is JOY for the redeemed...They will enter the Heavenly City with singing; everlasting JOY will crown their heads. Gladness and JOY will overtake them, and sorrow and sighing will flee away.

Isaiah 35:10

Now to Him who is able to keep you from falling and to present you before His glorious presence without fault and with great joy –
to the only God our Savior
be glory, majesty, power and authority
now and forevermore! Amen.
Jude 24-25

Truths On

Praise

But you are a chosen people, a royal priesthood, a holy nation, a people belonging to God, that you may declare the PRAISES of Him who called you out of darkness into His wonderful light.

1 Peter 2:9

I will extol the Lord at all times; His PRAISE will always be on my lips. My soul will boast in the Lord; let the afflicted hear and rejoice. Glorify the Lord with me; let us exalt His name together.

Psalm 34:1-3

Shout with joy to God, all the earth! Sing the glory of His name; make His PRAISE glorious! Say to God, "How awesome are Your deeds! So great is Your power that Your enemies cringe before You. All the earth bows down to You; they sing praise to You, they sing PRAISE to Your name."

Psalm 66:1-4

But as for me, I will always have hope; I will PRAISE You more and more. My mouth will tell of Your righteousness, of Your salvation all day long, though I know not its measure. I will come and pro-claim Your mighty acts, O Sovereign Lord; I will proclaim Your righteousness, Yours alone.

Psalm 71:14-16

PRAISE the Lord. Sing to the Lord a new song, his PRAISE in the as-sembly of the saints. Let them PRAISE His name with dancing and make music to Him with tambourine and harp. For the Lord takes delight in His people; He crowns the humble with salvation.

Psalm 149:1,3-4

Yours, O Lord, is the greatness and the power and the glory and the majesty and the splendor, for everything in heaven and earth is Yours. Yours, O Lord, is the kingdom; You are exalted as head over all... In Your hands are strength and power to exalt and give strength to all. Now, our God, we give You thanks, and PRAISE Your glorious name.

1 Chronicles 29:11,13

Praise be to the God and Father of our Lord Jesus Christ, who has blessed us in the heavenly realms with every spiritual blessing in Christ... In Him we were also chosen... in order that we, who were the first to hope in Christ, might be for the PRAISE of His glory.

Ephesians 1:3,11a, 12

Then I heard every creature in heaven and on earth and under the earth
and on the sea, and all that is in them, singing:
"To Him who sits on the throne and to the Lamb
be praise and honor and glory and power,
for ever and ever!"

Revelations 5:1

Promises On
Rest

My soul finds REST in God only; my salvation comes from Him. He alone is my rock and my salvation; He is my fortress, I will not be shaken.

Psalm 62:1-2

Thank you, Lord, that he who dwells in the shelter of the Most High will REST in the shadow of the Almighty. Therefore, I will say of the Lord, "You are my refuge and my fortress, my God in whom I trust."

Psalm 91:1-2

Let the beloved of the Lord REST secure in Him, for He shields him all day long, and the one the Lord loves RESTS between His shoulders.

Deuteronomy 33:12

This is what the Sovereign Lord says, "In repentance and REST is your salvation, in quietness and trust is your strength."

Isaiah 10:15

Now arise, O Lord God, and come to your RESTING place, You and the ark of Your might. May Your priests, O Lord God, be clothed with salvation, may Your saints rejoice in Your goodness.

2 Chronicles 6:41

Be at REST once more, O my soul, for the Lord has been good to you.

Psalm 116:7

This is what the Lord says, "Stand at the crossroads and look; ask for the ancient paths, ask where the good way is and walk in it, and you will find REST for your souls."

Jeremiah 6:16

There remains, then, a Sabbath-rest for the people of God; for anyone who enters God's REST also rests from his own work, just as God did from His. Let us, therefore, make every effort to enter that REST.

Hebrews 4:9-11

Be still and know that I am God. I will be exalted among the nations, I will be exalted in the earth.

Psalm 46:10

Come to Me, all who are weary and burdened,
and I will give you rest.
Take My yoke upon you and learn from Me,
for I am gentle and humble in heart,
and you will find rest for your souls.
For My yoke is easy and My burden is light.
Matthew 11:28-30

Promises On

Strength

Happy are those who hear the joyful call to worship, for they will walk in the light of Your presence, Lord. They rejoice all day long in Your wonderful reputation. They exult in Your righteousness. You are their glorious STRENGTH. It pleases You to make us STRONG.

Psalm 89:15-17 (NLT)

Whom have I in heaven but You? I desire You more than anything on earth. My health may fail, and my spirit may grow weak, but God remains the STRENGTH of my heart; He is mine forever.

Psalm 73:25-26 (NLT)

The Lord is my light and my salvation—whom shall I fear? The Lord is the STRONGHOLD of my life—of whom shall I be afraid?

Psalm 27:1

Give thanks to the Lord, call on His name; make known among the nations what He has done. Sing to Him, sing praise to Him; tell of all His wonderful acts. Glory in His holy name; let the hearts of those who seek the Lord rejoice. Look to the Lord and His STRENGTH; seek His face always.

1 Chronicles 16:8-11

But I will sing of Your STRENGTH, in the morning I will sing of Your love; for You are my fortress, my refuge in times of trouble. O my STRENGTH, I sing praise to You; You, O God, are my fortress, my loving God.

Psalm 59:16-17

I have learned the secret of being content in any and every situation, whether well fed or hungry, whether living in plenty or in want. I can do everything through Him who gives me STRENGTH.

Philippians 4:12b-13

Finally, be STRONG in the Lord and in His mighty power. Put on the full armor of God so that you can take your stand against the devil's schemes.

Ephesians 6:10-11

He will keep you strong to the end,
so that you will be blameless
on the day of our Lord Jesus Christ.
God, who has called you into fellowship
with His Son Jesus Christ our Lord, is faithful.
1 Corinthians 1:8-9

Truths On

Suffering And Glory

We see Jesus, who was made a little lower than the angels, now crowned with GLORY and honor because He SUFFERED death, so that by the grace of God He might taste death for everyone.

Hebrews 2:9

In bringing many sons to GLORY, it was fitting that God, for whom and through whom everything exists, should make the author of their salvation perfect through SUFFERING.

Hebrews 2:10

Now if we are children, then we are heirs—heirs of God and co-heirs with Christ, if indeed we share in His SUFFERINGS in order that we may also share in His GLORY. I consider that our present SUFFERINGS are not worth comparing with the GLORY that will be revealed in us.

Romans 8:17-18

Therefore we do not lose heart. Though outwardly we are wasting away, yet inwardly we are being renewed day by day. For our light and momentary troubles are achieving for us an eternal GLORY that far outweighs them all. So we fix our eyes not on what is seen, but on what is unseen. For what is seen is temporary, but what is unseen is eternal.

2 Corinthians 4:16-18

In this you greatly rejoice, though now for a little while you may have had to SUFFER grief in all kinds of trials. These have come so that your faith of greater worth than gold.... may be proved genuine and may result in praise, GLORY and honor when Jesus Christ is revealed.... though you do not see Him now, you believe in Him and are filled with an inexpressible and glorious joy, for you are receiving the goal of your faith, the salvation of your souls.

1 Peter 1:6-9

Dear friends, do not be surprised at the painful trial you are SUFFERING, as though something strange were happening to you. But rejoice that you participate in the SUFFERINGS of Christ, so that you may be overjoyed when His GLORY is revealed.

1 Peter 4:12-13

And the God of all grace, who called you to His eternal GLORY in Christ, after you have SUFFERED a little while, will himself restore you and make you strong, firm and steadfast. To Him be the power for ever and ever. Amen.

1 Peter 5:10-11

Father, I want those You have given me
to be with me where I am, and to see My glory,
the glory you have given Me because
You loved Me before the creation of the world.
John 17:24

Prayers Of
Thanksgiving

Thank You God that Your divine power has given us everything we need for life and godliness through our knowledge of Him who called us by His own glory and goodness.

1 Peter 1:3

Thank You that we are able to fix our eyes not on what is seen, but what is unseen. For what is seen is temporary, but what is unseen is eternal.

2 Cor. 4:18

Thank You my Sovereign God, that You are able to do immeasurably more than all that I ask or imagine according to Your great power that is at work in Your people.

Ephesians 3:20

Thank You Lord that all things are possible to those who believe.

Mark 10:27

Thank You that You will keep in perfect peace Him whose mind is steadfast because He trusts in You.

Isaiah 26:3

Thank You for telling us Lord, not to be anxious for anything, but by prayer and petition, with thanksgiving, to present our requests to You. And Your peace - which transcends all understanding - will guard our hearts and minds in Christ Jesus.

Philippians 4:6-7

Thank You for your words to Jairus before you raised His daughter back to life, "Don't be afraid, just believe."

Luke 8:50

Thank You for Your promise that out of Your glorious riches You will strengthen me with power through Your Spirit in my inner being, that Christ may dwell in my heart through faith. And being rooted and grounded in love, I will be able to comprehend with all the saints how wide and long and high and deep is the love of Christ. For to know this love surpasses all knowledge and Your desire is that I would be filled to the measure of all the fullness of God.

Ephesians 3:16-19

But thanks be to God! He gives us the victory
through our Lord Jesus Christ.
Therefore stand firm. Let nothing move you.
1 Corinthians 15:57-58

Promises On

Trust

When I am afraid, I will TRUST in You. In God, whose word I praise, in God I TRUST; I will not be afraid. What can mortal man do to me?

Psalm 56:3-4

To You, O Lord, I lift up my soul; in You I TRUST, O my God.

Psalm 25:1-2

Those who know Your name will TRUST in you, for You, Lord, have never forsaken those who seek You.

Psalm 9:10

We wait in hope for You, Lord; You are our help and our shield. In You our hearts rejoice, for we TRUST in Your Holy Name.

Psalm 33:20-21

Lord, You lifted me out of the slimy pit, out of the mud and mire; You set my feet on a rock and gave me a firm place to stand. You put a new song in my mouth, a hymn of praise to our God. Many will see and fear and put their TRUST in the Lord.

Psalm 40:2-3

You will keep in perfect peace him whose mind is steadfast, because he TRUSTS in You. TRUST in the Lord forever, for the Lord, the Lord, is the Rock eternal.

Isaiah 26:3-4

TRUST in the Lord with all your heart and lean not on your own understanding; in all your ways acknowledge Him, and He will make your paths straight.

Proverbs 3:5-6

In Him you also TRUSTED, after you heard the word of truth, the gospel of your salvation; in whom also, having believed, you were sealed with the Holy Spirit of promise, who is the guarantee of our inheritance until the redemption of the purchased possession, to the praise of His glory.

Ephesians 1:13-14

(Jesus said) - Do not let your hearts be troubled. TRUST in God; TRUST also in Me.

John 14:1

I will trust in Your unfailing Love forever and ever.
I will praise You forever
for what You have done; In Your name
I will hope, for Your name is good.
Psalm 52:8b-9

Endnotes

CHAPTER ONE

1. Paul E. Billheimer, *Don't Waste Your Sorrows* (Fort Washington: Christian Literature Crusade, Inc., 1977), 31.

CHAPTER TWO

1. Mike Bickle and Dana Candler, *The Rewards of Fasting* (Kansas City: Forerunner Books, 2005).

2. Lysa TerKeurst, *Made to Crave: Satisfying Your Deepest Desire with God, Not Food* (Grand Rapids: Zondervan, 2010).

CHAPTER THREE

1. Dr. and Mrs. Howard Taylor, *Hudson Taylor's Spiritual Secret* (Chicago: Moody Press, 1989) 172.

2. Ibid, 177.

CHAPTER FIVE

1. Sylvia Gunter, "You Don't Need an Apology — You Need God" *The Father's Business*, accessed October 3, 2012, http://www.thefathersbusiness.com/devotionals.php.

CHAPTER EIGHT

1. Tim Hansel, *You Gotta Keep Dancin'* (Elgin, IL: David C. Cook, 1985) 132.

2. Stephen M. Miller, "The Horrors of Roman Crucifixion" accessed October 11, 2012, http://www.lillenas.com/vcmedia/2401/2401385.pdf.

3. Julia Duin, "When God Speaks in a Whisper" *Charisma Magazine*, September 2001, 62.

4. *Life Without Limbs*; "About Nick" accessed October 11, 2012, http://www.lifewithoutlimbs.org/about-nick/.

CHAPTER TEN

1. Ray Pritchard, *The God You Can Trust* (Eugene, OR: Harvest House, 2003), 53.

2. Ibid, 53.

3. Robert Rogers and Stan Finger, *Into the Deep* (Carol Stream, IL: Tyndale House Publishers, 2007), 163-164.

4. Capt. Dale Black, *Flight to Heaven* (Grand Rapids: Bethany House Publishers, 2010), 99-100.

CHAPTER ELEVEN

1. Paul E. Billheimer, *Don't Waste Your Sorrows* (Fort Washington: Christian Literature Crusade, Inc., 1977), 70.

2. Lee Strobel, "Why Does God Allow Tragedy and Suffering?" *BibleGatewayBlog*, accessed October 13, 2012, http://www.biblegateway.com/blog/2012/07/why-does-god-allow-tragedy-and-suffering/.

Author and Ministry Information

Rev. Sally A. Keiran

Dunamis International Ministries

To schedule Sally for a speaking engagement or for more information on their ministry, Visit:

www.dunamis7.com
Email: *preparehisway@gmail.com*

☙

CPSIA information can be obtained at www.ICGtesting.com
Printed in the USA
BVOW04s1924190713

325906BV00007B/31/P